NEW HODDER ENGLISH

Sue Hackman • Alan Howe • Patrick Scott

3

Hodder & Stoughton

A MEMBER OF THE HODDER HEADLINE GROUP

ACKNOWLEDGEMENTS

The publishers would like to thank the following contributors:

Bernadette Fitzgerald	–	Unit One *Biography*
Jean Moore and John Catron	–	Unit Two *Gothic Horror*,
		Unit Six, *Writing Wrongs*,
		Unit Seven *Poetry Backpack*
Jo Shackleton	–	Unit Three *Macbeth*
Jan Malt	–	Unit Four *Investigating Narrative Texts*,
		Unit Five *Investigating Non-Narrative Texts*

Edited by Kevin Eames

Copyright Text:

p18 *Nanny* © Noel Hill; p21 'Carrey on Laughing' © 1995 Smash Hits; p22 'Janet Marsh's Biography' from *Nature Diary* © Penguin; p22 'Paolo Maldini' © Football Italia; p46 *The Attic* © T S Rae, HarperCollins; p80 *I Know Why the Caged Bird Sings* by Maya Angelou, Virago Press, 1993; p80 *Night* by Elie Wiesel, Penguin Books, 1981; p82 *Hacker* by Malorie Blackman © Oneta Malorie Blackman 1992, published by Doubleday. A division of Transworld Publishers. All rights reserved; p83 *The Hitch Hiker's Guide to the Galaxy* by Douglas Adams, Heinemann, 1995; p83 *The Throttlepenny Murder* by Roger J Green, OUP, 1999; p84 *Northern Lights* by Philip Pullman, reprinted with kind permission of Scholastic Ltd; p85 *The Ghost Messengers* by Robert E. Swindells, Collins Educational, 1988; p104 'Warning: Delays likely, iguana ahead' originally published in the *Daily Mail* 27.7.99, reproduced by kind permission of the *Daily Mail*; p106 'Ali's Treetop Tiger Tussle' reproduced from *Tales of Real Survival* by permission of Usborne Publishing, 83–85 Saffron Hill, London EC1N 8RT © 1995 Usborne Publishing Ltd; p107 text taken from WaterAid leaflet; p109 *The Lost Continent* © Bill Bryson 1989, published by Black Swan, a division of Transworld Publishers. All rights reserved; p110 *AA Book of British Villages* published by Drive Publications Ltd (edited and designed by Reader's Digest Association Ltd); p117 extract A: *The Unusual Guide to Bath* by John Chadwick, published by Nigel J. Clarke Publications; p117 extract B: *Writing Home* by Alan Bennett, Faber & Faber Ltd; p117 Extract C: *The Lost Continent* © Bill Bryson 1989, published by Black Swan, a division of Transworld Publishers. All rights reserved; p118 extract D: taken from leaflet produced by the *English Heritage*; p118 extract E: originally published in the *Daily Mail* 27.4.95, reproduced by kind permission of the *Daily Mail*; p118 extract F: originally published in 'Poisoned by a Jellyfish' article in *Sugar* magazine; p119 extract G: (information about The Eagles) from *The Best of Rock* by Adam Clayson, published by Orion; p119 extract I: *The Industry Giant Manual* published by Interactive Magic; p143 'Hawk Roosting' © Ted Hughes, Faber & Faber Ltd; p148 'Roman Wall Blues' © W.H. Auden, Faber & Faber Ltd; p151 Song Lyrics, from *The Very Best of Leadbelly*, Kensington Music Ltd; p152 'The Man in the Bowler Hat' © A.S.J. Tessimond; p157 'A Hard Rain's A-Gonna Fall' song lyrics from *The Freewheelin'* album by Bob Dylan, 1963 © 1963, renewed in 1991 Special Rider Music.

Copyright Photographs:

p15 Harold Wilson © Topham Picture Point; p18 'Nanny' © Noel Hill; p21 Jim Carrey © The Ronald Grant Archive; p42 Gothic Wedding © Press Association/Topham; p42 Gargoyles © J. Allan Cash Ltd; p50 © Puffin Book Club; p70 *Ellen Terry as Lady Macbeth*, 1889, by John Singer Sargent © Tate Gallery, London, 1999; p107 Photo on Water Aid Leaflet © Mark Edwards/Still Pictures; p109 Cover of *The Lost Continent* by Bill Bryson, cover illustrations © David Cook, published by Black Swan, a division of Transworld Publishers, 1999; p110 Cover of *The AA Book of British Villages* © 1980 Drive Publications Ltd; p112 Caged animal © Jean-Luc Zeigler/Still Pictures; p113 Roaming Lion © M. & C. Denis-Hoot/Still Pictures; p146 Saddam Hussein © AKG Photo, London; p146 Adolf Hitler. From Illustrated London News; p146 People in demonstration © Associated Press/Armando Franca; p146 Athlete © Actionplus/Glyn Kirk; p146 Pope in crowd © Uittoriano rastelli/Corbis; p151 Leadbelly © Bettmann/Corbis; p154 *The Son of Man*, 1964, Rene Magritte © The Bridgeman Art Library Private Collection, London, copyright ADAGP, Paris and DACS, London 2001; p156 Kosovo Refugees in Macedonia © Associated Press/Eric Draper; p156 Turkish Earthquake © Associated Press/Murad Sezer; p156 War in Chechnya © Associated Press/Maxim Marmur; p157 Bob Dylan © AKG Photo, London.

Every effort has been made to trace copyright holders of material reproduced in this book. Any rights not acknowledged here will be acknowledged in subsequent printings if notice is given to the publisher.

A CIP record for this title is available from the British Library.

ISBN   0 340 77538 6

First published 2001

Impression number	10 9 8 7 6 5 4 3 2
Year	2006 2005 2004 2003 2002 2001

Copyright © 2001 Sue Hackman, Alan Howe and Patrick Scott

Typesetting and page design by Christopher Halls.

Printed in Italy for Hodder & Stoughton Educational, a division of Hodder Headline plc, 338 Euston Road, London NW1 3BH.

INTRODUCTION

Welcome to *New Hodder English*. This course book and its two companions represent a quality English curriculum for Key Stage 3 (S1–3). It meets the demands of the recently revised National Curriculum (and Scottish 5–14 guidelines) without compromising on range, quality literature and a progressive ethos. Reading, writing and speaking and listening are integrated. Particular efforts have been made to provide accessible older literature, gripping non-fiction and opportunities to foreground speaking and listening.

STRUCTURE OF THE BOOK

This book consists of five units, each covering approximately half a term of work. In the final half term, two additional mini-units have been provided to maintain pace and interest and to prepare pupils for the following year. The units are arranged to establish, revisit and consolidate key skills, and over the period of a year, all teaching points are revisited in new contexts. This course provides a full curriculum for those who wish to use it that way, but it is also a flexible resource. The units can be enhanced with texts and materials that schools have found successful, or organised around existing programmes of work.

LANGUAGE SKILLS

Language skills are developed in three ways. Firstly, each coursebook contains a unit devoted directly to language skills, and all the others take as their topic a linguistic or literary focus. Secondly, every opportunity is taken to teach language conventions at the time they are required in context. At these points, the conventions are taught directly and explicitly. Thirdly, it is assumed that teachers will continue to support pupils by giving them feedback on the detail of their writing, and specific support is provided in the Help Boxes.

STRUCTURE OF UNITS

Each unit is prefaced by a statement of aims, so that pupils have a sense of why they are undertaking the work. The activities in the unit are designed to introduce new skills and knowledge, consolidate the key points of learning and then to explore and develop these key points. Most activities can be undertaken individually or in groups. As much room as possible has been left for teachers to organise the activities in their own way. Each unit concludes with suggestions for further work to extend the more able.

PROGRESSION

The coursebook has been designed to interest and develop pupils of a wide range of ability, and most schools will find it suitable for mixed ability classes. The intention is to provide a motivating and accessible way in to the full curriculum for all pupils, and to establish, consolidate and extend a handful of key learning points in each unit.

ASSESSMENT

Teachers should continue to use their usual patterns of assessment and recording, though the organisation of the course in units does lend itself to periodic review and a focus for assessment. Each unit contains focal writing assignments which will form one important strand of assessment. Importantly, teachers will be able to assess how far pupils have learnt new ideas and been able to use them in their own reading, writing and speaking. In the end, this is the only test of effective teaching and learning.

CONTENTS

UNIT ONE

Biography

The aims of this unit are to enable you to put together a factual account of someone else's life and to use a variety of techniques for gathering, selecting and writing up the information you require.

As you work through this unit you will develop your skills as:

SPEAKERS AND LISTENERS

by sharing ideas and debating controversial issues
by asking and answering questions, listening attentively and responding

READERS

by reading a range of factual and informative texts, noting their different styles and how they are organised
by selecting and comparing information from different sources

WRITERS

by taking notes in order to plan, draft and publish biographies
by writing a biography of your own

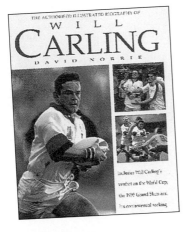

You probably know a lot about your best friend's life. You probably know a lot about the life of your favourite singer or sports personality. When you turn this page, you will begin to learn about biographies and, eventually, go on to write about your friend or your hero...

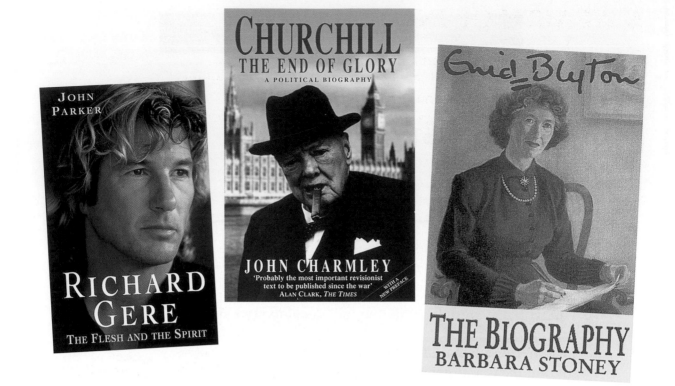

WHAT IS A BIOGRAPHY?

biography, noun, the story of a person's life written by someone else.
Oxford English Dictionary

What biographies have you heard about? Have you read any?

WHO'S CONCERNED?

- Working in groups, discuss the following questions. Make a note of your answers and share them with the class.

1 Why do authors write biographies?

2 What types of people have biographies written about them?

3 Why might people choose to read a biography?

4 What type of person would you like to read about? Why?

A WEALTH OF INFORMATION

A biography is full of facts about a person.

Think about all the information which has been written about you from the time you were born – medical records, school reports, letters, certificates, diaries. Some of them may be nothing more than scraps of paper, long since thrown away.

But they all say something about you – what you do, where you have been, how you were feeling...

YOUR LIFE – THE EVIDENCE

Make a list of sources of information about yourself like the chart shown here.

INFORMATION WRITTEN ABOUT ME		
Type of information	**Who reads it?** (audience)	**Why was it written?** (purpose)
School report	Me, parents, friend, tutor, Head of Year	To describe my behaviour and progress in school

GATHERING INFORMATION

Biographies gather information about their chosen subject in a wide variety of ways.

• reading letters and diaries

• interviewing

- reading newspaper articles

- studying photographs or paintings

- questioning other people who knew the person

- examining documents

Can you think of any difficulties that might arise with any of these methods of obtaining information? Why do you think most biographers prefer to use all these sources of information rather than relying on just one?

FACT OR OPINION?

Look carefully at some of the information which was written about a
boy called Kieran before his first birthday.

No fee is chargeable for this certificate

1 & 2 ELIZ. 2 CH. 20

GR805518

CERTIFICATE OF BIRTH

Name and Surname	Kieran Gabriel WILLIAMS
Sex	Male
Date of Birth	Eleventh April 1994
Place of Birth — Registration District	Bristol
Sub-district	Bristol

I, R A J Underwood   Deputy   Registrar of Births and Deaths
for the sub-district of Bristol   in the
Registration District of Bristol   do hereby
certify that the above particulars have been compiled from an entry in
a register in my custody.

Date   19/04/1994

PYI94E48

Raj Underwood
Registrar of Births and Deaths,
Deputy

CAUTION – It is an offence to falsify a certificate or to make or knowingly use a false certificate or a copy of a false certificate intending it to be accepted as genuine to the prejudice of any person, or to possess a certificate knowing it to be false without lawful authority.

WARNING: THIS CERTIFICATE IS NOT EVIDENCE OF THE IDENTITY OF THE PERSON PRESENTING IT

3 March 1995

The bath, Kieran… you love it!
Splish, splosh, splash! Your latest
joy is to try to drink your bath water,
lapping it up like a little puppy at a
puddle. With soap bubbles all over
your face, you are like Father Christmas!

Everything is material for your curious,
beautiful hands. You're very tactile,
enjoying the feel of : sand, soil, sponge,
paper, pasta. You explored your new
safety gates with your feet. You
used them like a ballet barre, testing
their strength and use of space with
your toes, like a dancer warming up…

```
             NURSERY REVIEW FORM


Name: Kieran Williams          Date: 22.2.95


D.o.b: 11.4.94


    SOCIAL & PERSONAL SKILLS

    Kieran is a very sociable little boy. He
    enjoys lots of contact with both his peers and
    familiar adults.

    He enjoys group sessions such as singing,
    music and movement, story time, and will
    participate by vocalising and clapping.

    He always likes to be near, but is still a
    little uneasy around the slightly more active
    children.

    Kieran enjoys the social aspect of meal times,
    and becomes very vocal.
```

KIERAN – THE EVIDENCE

- Working in pairs, discuss why you think each of these pieces of
  information was produced. Who might want, or need, to read each
  one? Which pieces of information do you think contain opinion as
  well as fact, and what helps you to decide?

A biography may contain opinion, untruths and biased information as
well as facts. As a reader, you need to be able to judge whether a
statement is based on fact or opinion in order to assess it as a piece of
evidence.

IS IT AUTHORISED?

A biography which is written with the permission of the person it is about is called an *authorised* biography.

However, there are other methods than those illustrated on pages 8–9 for obtaining information about a person.

A biographer who resorts to these methods is almost certainly working against the wishes of his or her subject. Access to many of the generally accepted sources of information has been denied. The result is an *unauthorised* biography.

The next time you are in a library or a bookshop, find the biography section. Browse through the biographies: see if you can discover which ones are authorised – and which are not. What might help you to decide?

WHOSE RIGHT?

- Working in groups, elect one member of the class to 'chair' a discussion and another to record the main points raised.

- Debate the following issues:

  'We have a right to know about the private lives of public figures in a democracy' (public figures might include politicians, pop stars, royalty).

  'Public figures have a right to keep their personal lives private; it should be made illegal for the Press to invade their privacy.'

- Now write a paragraph which clearly explains and justifies your view.

DIFFERENT TYPES OF BIOGRAPHY

A biography can be written about anyone, living or dead, famous or not.

On the next few pages are some examples of different types of biographical writing. As you read, think carefully about their similarities and differences. Make a note of any ideas or techniques that you think are interesting or useful. You may find them helpful when you start to write a biography for yourself.

OBITUARIES

When a famous person dies, biographies – obituaries – are produced about them on the radio, on television and in the newspapers.

When former prime minister Harold Wilson died in May 1995, obituaries about him filled a great many newspaper pages.

"He was a pretty good Prime Minister to work with. He was extremely courteous, mostly very kind... He was at his best when things were going badly"
Lord Jenkins of Hillhead

"Harold Wilson was one of the men who ruined post-war Britain. He was a small, posturing, visionless politician, personally pleasant to his friends and even to his enemies, amusing and irreverent and apparently kind. But his public work was a long strung-out disaster."
Hugo Young

"He was a very kind man, full of common sense. When people look at the balance of his contribution, it was enormous"
Tony Benn

"In the sixties Harold Wilson presided over Labour's greatest opportunity to achieve an irreversible shift towards democratic socialism. That opportunity was missed"
Billy Bragg, singer/songwriter

"He was not a politician with a very long social vision, but creating the Open University was a good attempt to harness the creative impulses he had"
Stuart Hall, professor of sociology at the Open University

WHO WANTS TO KNOW?

- Working with a partner, discuss which of these obituaries praises
  Harold Wilson. What criticisms are made? For what kind of
  audience do you think these obituaries were written?

LITERARY BIOGRAPHY

Biographies have always been popular. In the past, as now, they have often been lengthy books written by famous people about famous people. Important writers have themselves often become the subject of someone else's work.

Read the two extracts that follow about two famous poets. The first extract describes part of the difficult journey the poet John Clare made when he escaped from a mental institution.

Clare's flight from Dr. Allen's custody was accomplished by dint of extraordinary perseverance, involving an amount of physical suffering almost unexampled, and approaching starvation and the most horrible of deaths. The poet started early on the morning of the 20th of July, with not a penny in his pocket, and no other knowledge of the road than that given to him by a gipsy whom he had met a few days before. This gipsy at first promised more active assistance in his flight; but did not keep his word, owing, probably, to the inability of the poor lunatic to procure any tangible reward. However, urged onward by his intense desire to see his 'Mary' again, Clare did not hesitate to start alone on his unknown journey, and, groping his way along, like one wrapt in blindness, he at once succeeded so far as to get into the right track homewards. The first day he walked above twenty miles, to Stevenage, in Hertfordshire, where he arrived late at night, footsore and faint, having been without refreshment the whole day. He rested for the night in an old barn, on some trusses of clover, taking the singular precaution, before lying

down, of placing his head towards the north, so as to know in which direction to start the next morning. This day, the 21st of July, he rose early, pursuing his way northward, and crawling more than walking along the road. A man threw him a penny which he used to get a glass of ale; but beyond this he had again no refreshment. After a second night, spent in the open air, he rose once more to crawl onward, slowly but steadily. To stifle the torments of hunger, he now took to the frightful expedient of eating grass with the beasts in the field. The grass served to appease the dreadful pains of his stomach, yet left him in the same drowsy condition in which he was before. His feet were bleeding, the dry gravel of the road having penetrated his old worn-out shoes; but he heeded it not, and stedfastly pursued his way northward. Alternately sleeping and walking, sometimes wandering about in a circle, lying down in ditches at the roadside, and continuing to eat grass, together with a few bits of tobacco which he found in his pocket, he at length reached the neighbourhood of Peterborough and scenes familiar to his eye.

From *The Life of John Clare* by Frederick W. Martin

The second extract describes the death of the poet Wilfred Owen, who was killed within a few days of the end of the first world war.

With Captain Somerville in hospital, Wilfred Owen was still in command of D Company and, although saddened by news of the deaths first of Robbie Ross and then of Philip Bainbrigge, death now meant less to him than formerly. He no longer took the cigarette from his mouth as he wrote Deceased across the letter to be 'returned to sender'.

Early on the 18th October, Owen left the red tent shielded with corrugated iron that had been his billet and began the long march back towards the guns. The Germans were falling back, and a sense that the end was in sight no doubt contributed to Owen's good humour when, on the last evening of October, he wrote to his mother.

The night of the 3/4 November had been chosen for the crossing of the Sambre Canal. Rain fell until midnight and, when it stopped, a thick mist settled in the valley. When the minute hands touched 5.45 and the shrilling of many whistles was added to the thunder of the British barrage cratering the east bank of the Canal, Owen led his platoon over the dark, wet fields. Five minutes after zero, the barrage lifted and the assault troops in extended line moved down the last sloping field and, on planks and duckboards, scrambled over or through the flooded ditch. As they struggled up the last short slope to the muddy tow-path, the first men began to fall. The far bank bristled with German machine-guns, brought up as the British barrage lifted, and behind that parapet they kept up a scorching fire.

Through this hurricane the small figure of Owen walked backwards and forwards between his men, patting them on the shoulder, saying 'well done' and 'you're doing very well, my boy'. He was at the water's edge, giving a hand with some duckboards, when he was hit and killed. Seven days later, as the guns fell silent on the Western Front, the survivors piled their rifles, took off their helmets, and went to sleep; the living like the dead.

In Shrewsbury, the Armistice bells were ringing when the Owens' front door sounded its small chime, heralding the telegram that Tom and Susan had dreaded for two years.

Adapted from Wilfred Owen: a biography by Jon Stallworthy

THE BIOGRAPHER'S BIAS

It is difficult for a biographer not to reveal how he or she regards his or her subject.

- Working on your own, write about the attitudes of the authors of these two extracts towards their subjects. Make a note of quotations which support your views.

THE 'ORDINARY' PERSON'S STORY

Biographies are sometimes written about people who are not famous – though they may become famous if their biography is a best-seller!

So what makes a biography of someone we have never even heard of interesting to read?

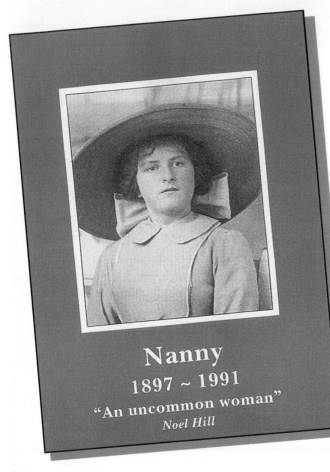

Nanny
1897 ~ 1991
"An uncommon woman"
Noel Hill

The extract that follows is from a biography called *Nanny* which the author, Noel Hill, wrote about his grandmother. Here he explains why he decided to write it and what he hopes his intended readers will gain from it.

To my brothers and sisters, their spouses, their children and grandchildren and their spouses; to my aunts and uncles and to my mother's closest friends, all of whom knew her well and loved her dearly. All were proud and privileged to be considered members of her family. I hope that each of you will find pleasure in reading Nanny's writings again. Keep this book as a memento of an uncommon woman who loved you all for what you were and not what you might have been.

SOMEONE YOU KNOW

- Discuss with a partner why an author might wish to write about someone who is not famous. Would you read this kind of biography? Why?

- Think of someone you know who would make a suitable subject for this kind of biography. Explain your choice to your partner.

INTERVIEWING

You will shortly begin to put together material for a biography of someone you know.
One of the most useful ways of gathering information about someone is to interview him or her.

These pages will help you to conduct a successful interview.

HELP

QUESTIONS, QUESTIONS

Good interviewing is not just about asking questions – it is about asking the right questions. You want your subject's answers to be as informative as possible.

The interviewer on the left has asked a 'closed' question, and receives a one-word answer.

However, the interviewer on the right has asked an 'open' question, and receives a full explanation.

OPEN OR CLOSED?

- With your partner, decide if the following questions are 'open' or 'closed'?

  1 What time is it?

  2 Why do you think that pupils are required to wear school uniform?

  3 What's your favourite colour?

4 How would you spend your dream holiday?

- Try making up some of your own 'open' and 'closed' questions about school life, and ask your partner to answer them. Were you right?

WHAT MAKES AN INTERVIEW SUCCESSFUL?

- Working in groups, compile a list of suggestions for how to be a successful interviewer. Role play being a good and a bad interviewer, to help you make your list.

- Produce a sheet of advice on 'How to Conduct a Successful Interview'. Include advice on: preparation, tone of voice, body language, facial expression, type of questions.

- Before you write out your final draft, think about layout and presentation. How could you set out your draft to have the maximum impact on your reader?

The following points made by a group of students should give you a few ideas:

- Look interested in what is being said.

- Ask interesting questions that will get you 'good' open answers.

- Be prepared; do research on your subject.

- Respect the subject's privacy. They don't have to answer your questions and you're lucky to get the chance to interview them.

You may find it helpful to refer back to these guidelines as you read through the rest of this book.

WRITING A SHORT BIOGRAPHY

The following extracts are all short biographies. As you read them, think about the type of publication in which each piece may have first appeared, and the style in which each of the three is written.

CARREY ON LAUGHING!

Most people think Jim Carrey just drifted out of nowhere and became an overnight filmstar in *Ace Ventura: Pet Detective*. Wrong!

- His full name is James Eugene – Eugene! – Carrey. He's 32 years old, Canadian and says about his success that, "I deserve it as much as the next guy."

- He once played Santa in his school's Christmas show when he was nine. Apparently the beard kept falling off.

- Unfortunately, when he moved up to high school, he was Jim "No Mates" Carrey. "I never had a friend in the world till I started hamming it up in class," he says.

- When he was young his whole family lived in a VW camper, then, when they became a bit flasher, they moved to a tent pitched on a friend's lawn.

- He's got a bit more cash in his wallet nowadays. Last year he bought a mansion in Hollywood for $3million complete with its own full-time butler.

PAOLO MALDINI

The son of the former Milan captain, Cesare Maldini, has not only continued the family tradition, but he has also eclipsed his famous father's notable achievements. Paolo Maldini had already made his Serie A debut for Milan by the time he was sixteen, and he recently celebrated the tenth anniversary of his first League appearance.

At 18, he was an Under-21 international and by 19 he played his first game for the Azzurri's senior side.

Maldini junior has since won a host of honours, including four League championship medals, and has played more than 60 times for his country.

Considering his tender years, the stylish defender certainly has time to overtake Dino Zoff's record of 112. Standing over six feet, Maldini adds immense power and pace to his outstanding technique. Without any question, Paolo Maldini is the finest left-back in the world today.

Janet Marsh

Janet Marsh, born in 1953, grew up in a small village in Sussex, but has been painting and studying the natural life of the Itchen Valley in Hampshire since the age of fourteen. In London, she attended the Byam Shaw School of Art, Camberwell School of Arts and Crafts, and finally the Royal College of Art, where she studied natural history illustration and obtained her MA. Her paintings have been featured in the *Sunday Telegraph* and *Sunday Times* magazines, and been bought for Prince Philip's collection.

DO IT YOURSELF

- Write a list of questions you could ask somebody about school, such as questions about their option choices, feelings about school, likes and dislikes. Try to have at least six 'open' questions on your list.

- Ask a partner your questions, remembering the advice you have already written on how to conduct a successful interview.

- Make brief notes of the answers.

- In about 150 words, write up these answers into a brief biographical account.

- Before you produce your final version, ask your subject to read your draft to check that the information is accurate.

You might like to combine your brief biographical pieces into a class yearbook. A copy could be placed in your school library.

WRITING A FULL BIOGRAPHY

You are now going to write a full biography of someone you know well. The following stages should result in a thoughtfully-presented informative piece of work.

PLANNING

Choose the person you are going to write about. It should be someone:

you know well (friend, relation)

you would enjoy interviewing

you will be able to interview within the next week

who has the time to talk to you

who will allow you to write about him or her

Write a list of possible chapter headings to include in the biography, based on what you already know about the person – choose just one of the chapter headings to write about, and put an asterisk by it.

Write down between ten and fifteen questions which are relevant for the chapter you have chosen to write. Remember to make most of them 'open' questions.

List any other sources of information which you will collect, such as interviews with other people who know your subject; letters; diaries; photographs; newspaper cuttings; a family tree.

Fix a date and a suitable time for your interview with your subject. Decide if you will write down the answers you are given or if you will tape them.

THE INTERVIEW

You will probably find it helpful to refer back to the list you compiled on successful interviewing on page 20.

PRESENTATION

Think very carefully about what you will put on the front and back covers. What title will you give your biography? Try to make your title eyecatching. One student entitled her biography about her practical joker grandfather, who is a dentist: *Fangs for the Memories.*

Would you like to write a dedication at the front? What will it say?

Write a final list of chapter headings, based on the information you now have about your subject. Try to make the headings interesting as well as informative – they should make someone want to read your work. Put an asterisk against the chapter you are writing.

Other features a biographer can use to help the reader include sub-headings within each chapter, an index, a glossary, photographs or illustrations with captions, and even different types and sizes of print.

You might find it helpful to look at several different biographies, noting how other authors have made use of these features, before you work them into your own biography.

WRITING YOUR BIOGRAPHY

Now write your draft for your chosen chapter.

HELP

GRAMMAR GUIDELINES

As you write your draft remember to use the following biographical techniques:

- third person pronouns – *she* or *he* – not *I*
  example: Her childhood was a happy one.

- the past tense of verbs
  example: He joined the army – *not* He joins the army.

- reported speech
  example: My Aunt Meg explained that she enjoyed her first day at school – *not* 'I enjoyed my first day at school,' said Aunt Meg.

Occasionally, you could quote the exact words your subject said, for special effect. *Example*: 'I'll never forget that bomb dropping on our house!' she told me.

Read through your final draft. Check that your spellings and punctuation are perfect.

If possible, let your subject read through your draft, to make sure that all of your information is correct; make any necessary changes.

Now produce your final 'good' copy. This could be written by hand, typed or produced on a word-processor.

WHAT NEXT?

During this unit you have looked at types of source material for biographies, different methods for gathering this material and a variety of biographical forms within which to write up an account of someone's life. You have planned and written a biography of someone you know, using the skills you have developed.

This unit, perhaps more than any of the others in this book, has exercised your skills as a listener during the interviews that you have carried out.

However, many biographies are written about people who have been dead for long time. Authors cannot always listen to their subject's life stories and must therefore rely more heavily on other skills. What do you think are the most important qualities in a biographer who can never meet or speak with his or her subject?

You may wish to follow up your study of biography by trying the following project:

- Choose one of your favourite stars – you might choose an actor, a singer, a sports personality – and collect as much information about that person as you can. (Remember that the more famous the person, the easier it will be to find useful information.)

  Compile a scrapbook or collage of the material you have collected, including photographs. For each piece of material, write in where it came from and the date (if you have it) and then your own comments on that piece of information or picture.

  Write a short biography about the person you chose (no more than a page), based on your collection.

  Present your scrapbook/collage to other members of your group, talking them through your biographical collection.

Gothic Horror

If you work systematically through this unit, your findings will contribute towards a class display about all aspects of the Gothic –
a GOTHIC COLLAGE – and you will develop your skills as:

SPEAKERS AND LISTENERS

by discussing a horror story, making predictions and observations
by using drama to explore the thoughts and feelings of characters
by finding the most effective way of telling your own horror stories

READERS

by reading one complete short story and extracts from other stories
by identifying common elements of 'Gothic horror'
by studying the techniques used by the writers

WRITERS

by learning how to make notes about the key points in a text
by presenting your research findings about 'Gothic horror'
by imitating the style of horror writers in your own work.

The wind howled around the great mansion. Distantly, the church clock tolled the hours. As if possessed, Algernon Blackwood's quill pen scratched the closing words of the story he was working on.

Read it, if you dare...

A SHORT STORY

by Algernon Blackwood

When the words 'Not Guilty' sounded through the crowded courtroom that dark December afternoon, Arthur Wilbraham, the great criminal KC, and leader for the triumphant defence, was represented by his junior; but Johnson, his private secretary, carried the verdict across to his chambers like lightning.

'It's what we expected, I think,' said the barrister, without emotion; 'and, personally, I am glad the case is over.' There was no particular sign of pleasure that his defence of John Turk, the murderer, on a plea of insanity, had been successful, for no doubt he felt, as everybody who had watched the case felt, that no man had ever better deserved the gallows.

'I'm glad too,' said Johnson. He had sat in the court for ten days watching the face of the man who had carried out with callous detail one of the most brutal and cold-blooded murders of recent years.

The counsel glanced up at his secretary. They were more than employer and employed; for family and other reasons, they were friends. 'Ah, I remember; yes,' he said with a kind smile, 'and you want to get away for Christmas? You're going to skate and ski in the Alps, aren't you? If I was your age I'd come with you.'

Johnson laughed shortly. He was a young man of twenty-six, with a delicate face like a girl's. 'I can catch the morning boat now,' he said; 'but that's not the reason I'm glad the trial is over. I'm glad it's over because I've seen the last of that man's dreadful face. It positively haunted me. That white skin, with the black hair brushed low over the forehead, is a thing I shall never forget, and the description of the way the dismembered body was crammed and packed with lime into that—'

'Don't dwell on it, my dear fellow,' interrupted the other, looking at him curiously out of his keen eyes, 'don't think about it. Such pictures have a trick of coming back when one least wants them.' He paused a moment. 'Now go,' he added presently, 'and enjoy your holiday. I shall want all your energy for my Parliamentary work when you get back. And don't break your neck skiing.'

Johnson shook hands and took his leave. At the door he turned suddenly.

'I knew there was something I wanted to ask you,' he said. 'Would you mind lending me one of your kit-bags? It's too late to get one tonight, and I leave in the morning before the shops are open.'

'Of course; I'll send Harry over with it to your rooms. You shall have it the moment I get home.'

'I promise to take great care of it,' said Johnson gratefully, delighted to think that within thirty hours he would be nearing the brilliant sunshine of the high Alps in winter. The thought of that criminal court was like an evil dream in his mind.

He dined at his club and went on to Bloomsbury, where he occupied the top floor in one of those old, gaunt houses in which the rooms are large and lofty. The floor below his own was vacant and unfurnished, and below that were other lodgers whom he did not know. It was cheerless, and he looked forward heartily to a change. The night was even more cheerless: it was miserable, and few people were about. A cold, sleety rain was driving down the streets before the keenest east wind he had ever felt. It howled dismally among the big, gloomy houses of the great squares, and when he reached his rooms he heard it whistling and shouting over the world of black roofs beyond his windows.

In the hall he met his landlady, shading a candle from the draughts with her thin hand. 'This come by a man from Mr Wilbr'im's, sir.'

She pointed to what was evidently the kit-bag, and Johnson thanked her and took it upstairs with him. 'I shall be going abroad in the morning for ten days, Mrs Monks,' he said. 'I'll leave an address for letters.'

'And I hope you'll 'ave a merry Christmas, sir,' she said, in a raucous, wheezy voice that suggested spirits, 'and better weather than this.'

'I hope so too,' replied her lodger, shuddering a little as the wind went roaring down the street outside.

WHAT HAPPENS NEXT?

With a partner, look back over the text of the story so far:

- Who are the characters and what has happened to them up to this point?

- Do you find anything puzzling? Make a list of any questions that you would put to the author if you could.

- What do you think is likely to happen next? Make a record of what you think but keep it to yourselves. For example:

What might happen?	Evidence
John Turk will *go berserk*	He has been acquitted on the grounds of 'insanity'
	He has a 'dreadful' face — 'white skin with black hair brushed low'

When he got upstairs he heard the sleet volleying against the window panes. He put his kettle on to make a cup of hot coffee, and then set about putting a few things in order for his absence. 'And now I must pack – such as my packing is,' he laughed to himself, and set to work at once. He liked the packing, for it brought the snow mountains so vividly before him, and made him forget the unpleasant scenes of the past ten days. Besides, it was not elaborate in nature. His friend had lent him the very thing – a stout canvas kit-bag, sack-shaped, with holes round the neck for the brass bar and padlock. It was a bit shapeless, true, and not much to look at, but its capacity was unlimited, and there was no need to pack carefully. He shoved in his waterproof coat, his fur cap and gloves, his skates and climbing boots, his sweaters, snow-boots, and ear-caps; and then on top of those he piled his woollen shirts and underwear, his thick socks, puttees, and knickerbockers. The dress suit came next, in case the hotel people dressed for dinner, and then, thinking of the best way to pack his white shirts, he paused a moment to reflect. 'That's the worst of these kit-bags,' he mused vaguely, standing in the centre of the sitting-room, where he had come to fetch some string.

It was after ten o'clock. A furious gust of wind rattled the windows as though to hurry him up, and he thought with pity of the poor Londoners whose Christmas would be spent in such a climate, whilst he was skimming over snowy slopes in bright sunshine, and dancing in the evening with rosy-cheeked girls – Ah! that reminded him; he must put in his dancing pumps and evening socks. He crossed over from his sitting-room to the cupboard on the landing where he kept his linen.

And as he did so he heard someone coming softly up the stairs.

Handwritten margin notes:
- ① Looking forward to holiday
- ② Problems of Packing
- ③ Thinking of others compared with him

He stood still a moment on the landing to listen. It was Mrs Monk's step, he thought; she must be coming up with the last post. But then the steps ceased suddenly, and he heard no more. They were at least two flights down, and he came to the conclusion that they were too heavy to be those of his bibulous landlady. No doubt they belonged to a late lodger who had mistaken his floor. He went into his bedroom and packed his pumps and dress-shirts as best he could.

The kit-bag by this time was two-thirds full, and stood upright on its own base like a sack of flour. For the first time he noticed that it was old and dirty, the canvas faded and worn, and that it had obviously been subjected to rather rough treatment. It was not a very nice bag to have sent to him – certainly not a new one, or one that his chief valued. He gave the matter a passing thought, and went on with his packing. Once or twice, however, he caught himself wondering who it could have been wandering down below, for Mrs Monks had not come up with letters, and the floor was empty and unfurnished.

From time to time, moreover, he was almost certain he heard a soft tread of someone padding about over the bare boards – cautiously, stealthily, as silently as possible – and, further, that the sounds had been lately coming distinctly nearer. For the first time in his life he began to feel a little creepy. Then, as though to emphasize this feeling, an odd thing happened: as he left the bedroom, having just packed his recalcitrant white shirts, he noticed that the top of the kit-bag lopped over towards him with an extraordinary resemblance to a human face. The canvas fell into a fold like a nose and forehead, and the brass rings for the padlock just filled the position of the eyes. A shadow – or was it a travel stain? for he could not tell exactly – looked like hair. It gave him rather a turn, for it was so absurdly, so

Handwritten margin notes:

④ Housekeeper - last post.

⑤ Who was it?

⑥ Disappointed in kit bag condition

⑦ Still thinking about identity of person

⑧ Sounds are beginning to unsettle him

⑨ Shock at seeing "face"

outrageously, like the face of John Turk, the murderer.

He laughed and went into the front room, where the light was stronger. 'That horrid case has got on my mind,' he thought; 'I shall be glad of a change of scene and air.' In the sitting-room, however, he was not pleased to hear again that stealthy tread upon the stairs, and to realize that it was much closer than before, as well as unmistakably real. And this time he got up and went out to see who it could be creeping about on the upper staircase at so late an hour.

But the sound ceased; there was no one visible on the stairs. He went to the floor below, not without trepidation, and turned on the electric light to make sure that no one was hiding in the empty rooms of the unoccupied suite. There was not a stick of furniture large enough to hide a dog. Then he called over the banisters to Mrs Monks, but there was no answer, and his voice echoed down into the dark vault of the house, and was lost in the roar of the gale that howled outside. Everyone was in bed and asleep – everyone except himself and the owner of this soft and stealthy tread.

'My absurd imagination, I suppose,' he thought. 'It must have been the wind after all, although – it seemed so *very* real and close, I thought.' He went back to his packing. It was

by this time getting on towards midnight. He drank his coffee up and lit another pipe – the last before turning in.

It is difficult to say exactly at what point fear begins, when the causes of that fear are not plainly before the eyes. Impressions gather on the surface of the mind, film by film, as ice gathers upon the surface of still water, but often so lightly that they claim no definite recognition from the consciousness. Then a point is reached where the accumulated impressions become a definite emotion, and the mind realises that something has happened. With something of a start, Johnson suddenly recognised that he felt nervous – oddly nervous; also, that for some time past the causes of this feeling had been gathering slowly in his mind, but that he had only just reached the point where he was forced to acknowledge them.

It was a singular and curious malaise that had come over him, and he hardly knew what to make of it. He felt as though he were doing something that was strongly objected to by another person, another person, moreover, who had some right to object. It was a most disturbing and disagreeable feeling, not unlike the persistent promptings of conscience: almost, in fact, as if he were doing something he knew to be wrong. Yet, though he searched vigorously and honestly in his mind, he could nowhere lay his finger upon the secret of this growing

[Handwritten margin notes: 10 Explaining his reaction; (11) Unnerved by noise; 12 Still trying to explain his feelings; 13; (14) Searching his mind for exp. of his feelings of having done something wrong]

uneasiness, and it perplexed him. ⑮ *Fears growing*
More, it distressed and frightened
him.

'Pure nerves, I suppose,' he ⑯ *Trying to*
said aloud with a forced laugh. *laugh it off*
'Mountain air will cure all that!
Ah,' he added, still speaking to
himself, 'and that reminds me
– my snow-glasses.'

He was standing by the
door of the bedroom during
this brief soliloquy, and as
he passed quickly towards
the sitting-room to fetch
them from the cupboard
he saw out of the
corner of his eye the
distinct outline of a
figure standing on
the stairs, a few feet
from the top. It was
someone in a
stooping position,
with one hand
on the
banisters, and
the face
peering up
towards the
landing.

And at the same moment he heard a shuffling footstep. The person who had been creeping about below all this time had at last come up to his own floor. Who in the world could it be? And what in the name of Heaven did he want?

(17) Again wants to know who it is

Johnson caught his breath sharply and stood stock still. Then, after a few seconds' hesitation, he found his courage, and turned to investigate. The stairs, he saw to his utter amazement, were empty; there was no one. He felt a series of cold shivers run over him, and something about the muscles of his legs gave a little and grew weak. For the space of several minutes he peered steadily into the shadows that congregated about the top of the staircase where he had seen the figure, and then he walked fast – almost ran, in fact – into the light of the front room; but hardly had he passed inside the doorway when he heard someone come up the stairs behind him with a quick bound and go swiftly into his bedroom.

It was a heavy, but at the same time a stealthy footstep – the tread of somebody who did not wish to be seen. And it was at this

(18)

(19) Can't accept no-one is there

20 Now fearful.

precise moment that the nervousness he had hitherto experienced leaped the boundary line, and entered the state of fear, almost of acute, unreasoning fear. Before it turned into terror there was a further boundary to cross, and beyond that again lay the region of pure horror. Johnson's position was an unenviable one.

'By Jove! That was someone on the stairs, then,' he muttered, his flesh crawling all over; 'and whoever it was has now gone into my bedroom.' His delicate, pale face turned absolutely white and for some minutes he hardly knew what to think or do. Then he realized intuitively that delay only set a premium upon fear; and he crossed the landing boldly and went straight into the other room, where, a few seconds before, the steps had disappeared.

(21) Convincing himself someone is there

(22) Can't think

'Who's there? Is that you, Mrs Monks?' he called aloud, as he went, and heard the first half of his words echo down the empty stairs, while the second half fell dead against the curtains in a room that apparently held no other human figure than his own.

(23) Attempts to get a response

'Who's there?' he called again, in a voice unnecessarily loud and that only just held firm. 'What do you want here?'

(24) Very nervous.

THOUGHT TRACKING

- Look back over the last five pages of the story.

- Find two sentences that particularly help to increase the feeling of tension and suspense in the extract you just read. Explain why you chose them. You may find that your sentences are different to those chosen by other members of your group.

- What do you think is going through Johnson's mind? You can explore his innermost feelings as a group by tracking his thoughts through each stage of the story.

  Thought tracking is a technique that helps you, as a large group, imagine what a person is thinking and feeling.

- In groups, look back again over the last five pages. Pick out the sounds that are mentioned in the text. Think about how you could create sound effects to capture the noises described.

  You will need a volunteer to represent Johnson. The class should form a circle with 'Johnson' sitting or standing in the middle. Start by creating sound effects, and then voice Johnson's thoughts, either going round the circle one at a time or adding appropriate sentences and phrases as each individual thinks of something. To be successful, you will need to know the text well!

- Finally, look back at the predictions you made after reading the first two pages of the story. Have any of them come true? What do you predict will happen next?

'I'm sure I heard...'

'What was that?'

Sound effects e.g. footsteps

The curtains swayed very slightly, and, as he saw it, his heart felt as if it almost missed a beat; yet he dashed forward and drew them aside with a rush. A window, streaming with rain, was all that met his gaze. He continued his search, but in vain; the cupboards held nothing but rows of clothes, hanging motionless; and under the bed there was no sign of anyone hiding. He stepped backwards into the middle of the room, and, as he did so, something all but tripped him up. Turning with a sudden spring of alarm he saw – the kit-bag.

'Odd!' he thought. 'That's not where I left it!' A few moments before it had surely been on his right, between the bed and the bath; he did not remember having moved it. It was very curious. What in the world was the matter with everything? Were all his senses gone queer? A terrific gust of wind tore at the windows, dashing the sleet against the glass with the force of a small gunshot, and then fled away howling dismally over the waste of Bloomsbury roofs. A sudden vision of the Channel next day rose in his mind and recalled him sharply to realities.

'There's no one here at any rate; that's quite clear!' he exclaimed aloud. Yet at the time he uttered them he knew perfectly well that his words were not true and that he did not believe them himself. He felt exactly as though someone was hiding close about him, watching all his movements, trying to hinder his packing in some way. 'And two of my senses,' he added, keeping up the pretence, 'have played me the most absurd tricks: the steps I heard and the figure I saw were both entirely imaginary.'

He went back to the front room, poked the fire into a blaze, and sat down before it to think. What impressed him more than anything else was the fact that the kit-bag was no longer where he had left it. It had been dragged nearer to the door.

What happened afterwards that night happened, of course, to a man already excited by fear, and was perceived by a mind that had not the full and proper control, therefore, of the senses. Outwardly, Johnson remained calm and master of himself to the end, pretending to the very last that everything he witnessed had a natural explanation, or was merely delusions of his tired nerves. But inwardly, in his very heart, he knew all along that someone had been hiding downstairs in the empty suite when he came in, that this person had watched his opportunity and then stealthily made his way up to the bedroom, and that all he saw and heard afterwards, from the moving of the kit-bag to – well, to the other things this story has to tell – were caused directly by the presence of this invisible person.

And it was here, just when he most desired to keep his mind and thoughts controlled, that the vivid pictures received day after day upon the mental plates exposed in the courtroom of the Old Bailey, came strongly to light and developed themselves in the dark room of his inner vision. Unpleasant, haunting memories have a way of coming to life again just when the mind least desires them – in the silent watches of the night, on sleepless pillows, during the lonely hours spent by sick and dying beds. And so now, in the same way, Johnson saw nothing but the dreadful face of John Turk, the murderer, lowering at him from every corner of his mental field of vision; the white skin, the evil eyes, and the fringe of black hair low over the forehead. All the pictures of those ten days in court crowded back into his mind unbidden, and very vivid.

'This is all rubbish and nerves,' he exclaimed at length, springing with sudden energy from his chair. 'I shall finish my packing and go to bed. I'm overwrought, overtired. No doubt, at this rate I shall hear steps and things all night!'

But his face was deadly white all the same. He snatched up his field-glasses and walked across to the bedroom, humming a music-hall song as he went – a trifle too loud to be natural; and the instant he crossed the threshold and stood within the room something turned cold about his heart, and he felt that every hair on his head stood up.

The kit-bag lay close in front of him, several feet nearer to the door than he had left it, and just over its crumpled top he saw a head and face slowly sinking down out of sight as though someone were crouching behind it to hide, and at the same moment a sound like a long-drawn sigh was distinctly audible in the still air about him between the gusts of the storm outside.

Johnson had more courage and will-power than the girlish indecision of his face indicated; but at first such a wave of terror came over him that for some seconds he could do nothing but stand and stare. A violent trembling ran down his back and legs, and he was conscious of a foolish, almost hysterical, impulse to scream aloud. That sigh seemed in his very ear, and the air still quivered with it. It was unmistakably a human sigh.

'Who's there?' he said at length, finding his voice; but though he meant to speak with loud decision, the tones came out instead in a faint whisper, for he had partly lost control of his tongue and lips.

He stepped forward, so that he could see all around and over the kit-bag. Of course there was nothing there, nothing but the faded carpet and the bulging canvas sides. He put out his hands and threw open the mouth of the sack where it had fallen over, being only three parts full, and then he saw for the first time that round the inside, some six inches from the top, there ran a broad smear of dull crimson. It was an old and faded blood stain. He uttered a scream, and drew back his hands as if they had been burnt. At the same moment the kit-bag gave a faint, but unmistakable, lurch forward towards the door.

Johnson collapsed backwards, searching with his hands for the support of something solid, and the door, being further behind him than he realized, received his weight just in time to prevent his falling, and shut to with a resounding bang. At the same moment the swinging of his left arm accidentally touched the electric switch, and the light in the room went out.

It was an awkward and disagreeable predicament, and if Johnson had not been possessed of real pluck he might have done all manner of foolish things. As it was, however, he pulled himself together, and groped furiously for the little brass knob to turn the light on again. But the rapid closing of the door had set the coats hanging on it a-swinging, and his fingers became entangled in a confusion of sleeves and pockets, so that it was some moments before he found the switch. And in those few moments of bewilderment and terror two things happened that sent him beyond recall over the boundary into the region of genuine horror – he distinctly heard the kit-bag shuffling heavily across the floor in jerks, and close in front of his face sounded once again the sigh of a human being.

In his anguished efforts to find the brass button on the wall he nearly scraped the nails from his fingers, but even then, in those frenzied moments of alarm – so swift and alert are the impressions of a mind keyed-up by a vivid emotion – he had time to realize that he dreaded the return of the light, and that it might be better for him to stay hidden in the merciful screen of

darkness. It was but the impulse of a moment, however, and before he had time to act upon it he had yielded automatically to the original desire, and the room was flooded again with light.

But the second instinct had been right. It would have been better for him to stay in the shelter of the kind darkness. For there, close before him, bending over the half-packed kit-bag, clear as life in the merciless glare of the electric light, stood the figure of John Turk, the murderer. Not three feet from him the man stood, the fringe of black hair marked plainly against the pallor of the forehead, the whole horrible presentment of the scoundrel, as vivid as he had seen him day after day in the Old Bailey, when he stood there in the dock, cynical and callous, under the very shadow of the gallows.

In a flash Johnson realized what it all meant: the dirty and much-used bag; the smear of crimson within the top; the dreadful stretched condition of the bulging sides. He remembered how the victim's body had been stuffed into a canvas bag for burial, the ghastly, dismembered fragments forced with lime into this very bag; and the bag itself produced as evidence – it all came back to him as clear as day...

Very softly and stealthily his hand groped behind him for the handle of the door, but before he could actually turn it the very thing that he most of all dreaded came about, and John Turk lifted his devil's face and looked at him. At the same moment that heavy sigh passed through the air of the room, formulated somehow into words: 'It's my bag. And I want it.'

Johnson just remembered clawing the door open, and then falling in a heap on the floor of the landing, as he tried frantically to make his way into the front room.

He remained unconscious for a long time, and it was still dark when he opened his eyes and realized that he was lying, stiff and bruised, on the cold boards. Then the memory of what he had seen rushed back into his mind, and he promptly fainted again. When he woke the second time the wintry dawn was just beginning to peep in at the windows, painting the stairs a cheerless, dismal grey, and he managed to crawl into the front room, and cover himself with an overcoat in the armchair, where at length he fell asleep.

A great clamour woke him. He recognized Mrs Monk's voice, loud and voluble.

'What! You ain't been to bed, sir! Are you ill, or has anything 'appened? And there's an urgent gentleman to see you, though it ain't seven o'clock yet, and –'

'Who is it?' he stammered. 'I'm all right, thanks. Fell asleep in my chair, I suppose.'

'Someone from Mr Wilb'rim's, and he says he ought to see you quick before you go abroad, and I told him –'

'Show him up, please, at once,' said Johnson, whose head was whirling, and his mind was still full of dreadful visions.

Mr Wilbraham's man came in with many apologies, and explained briefly and quickly that an absurd mistake had been made, and that the wrong kit-bag had been sent over the night before.

'Henry somehow got hold of the one that came over from the courtroom, and Mr Wilbraham only discovered it when he saw his own lying in his room, and asked why it had not gone to you,' the man said.

'Oh!' said Johnson stupidly.

'And he must have brought you the one from the murder case instead, sir, I'm afraid,' the man continued, without the ghost of an expression on his face. 'The one John Turk packed the dead body in. Mr Wilbraham's awful upset about it, sir, and told me to come over first thing this morning with the right one, as you were leaving by the boat.'

He pointed to a clean-looking kit-bag on the floor, which he had just brought. 'And I was to bring the other one back, sir,' he added casually.

For some minutes Johnson could not find his voice. At last he pointed in the direction of his bedroom. 'Perhaps you would kindly unpack it for me. Just empty the things out on the floor.'

The man disappeared into the other room, and was gone for five minutes. Johnson heard the shifting to and fro of the bag, and the rattle of the skates and boots being unpacked.

'Thank you, sir,' the man said, returning with the bag folded over his arm. 'And can I do anything more to help you, sir?'

'What is it?' asked Johnson, seeing that he still had something he wished to say.

The man shuffled and looked mysterious. 'Beg pardon, sir, but knowing your interest in the Turk case, I thought you'd maybe like to know what's happened –'

'Yes.'

'John Turk killed hisself last night with poison immediately on getting his release, and he left a note for Mr Wilbraham saying as he'd be much obliged if they'd have him put away, same as the woman he murdered, in the old kit-bag.'

'What time – did he do it?' asked Johnson.

'Ten o'clock last night, sir, the warder says.'

POST MORTEM

- In groups, discuss how accurate your predictions were. Can you explain why they were correct or not? What does that tell you about the effect which the writer wanted to have?

- What do you think the title is?

FINDING THE PULSE OF FEAR

- Still in your group, identify the particular moments in the story when the tension builds and reaches its climax. If you are working in a large group you may find that the best way of doing this is by listing key quotations on a large sheet of paper.

- Use your ideas about the way in which Blackwood builds the tension in the story to complete the cardiograph (a graph showing measurement of the heart rate) and measure the fear felt by Johnson!

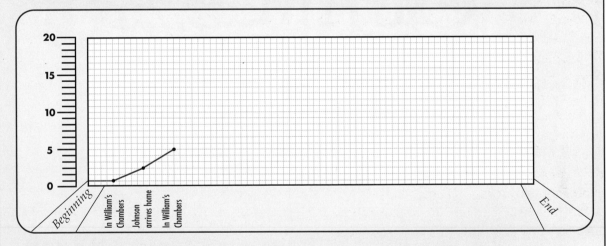

Plot the tension points along the bottom edge, using the scale on the left hand side of the screen and keeping a record of the quotations that do most to crank up the tension, as in the example below:

Page	Tension Builder	Score (/20)
1	'positively haunted me'	4

- When did **you** feel the tension begin to build? Did your level of fear follow the same line as that of your group? Use a different colour to plot in your own reaction to the story.

The title of the gothic horror story you have just read is The Kit-Bag.

WHAT IS 'GOTHIC'?

'Gothic' was first used to describe the pointed–arch style of medieval architecture. In the late eighteenth and early nineteenth centuries 'Gothic' was linked to the 'supernatural' or 'horror' fiction that became popular at that time, as much of the action took place in sinister castles with high, arched ceilings, or ruins and ancient graveyards.

Today, we use the term 'Gothic' to describe many things which have become associated with the supernatural and with elements of Gothic horror stories. Gothic images can be found in film and modern horror literature. 'Gothic' lettering is often used to suggest a connection with mystery, and 'Gothic' music and fashion have a cult following.

A GOTHIC COLLAGE (1)

The story of *The Kit-Bag* and the images in the Help box should help you to think about what is meant by 'Gothic'.

- Make a list of all the things that you associate with the word 'Gothic'.

- As a class, create your own collage display of Gothic images to add to the examples provided in this unit.

A GOTHIC COLLAGE (2)

- Working with a partner, explore any common elements that link *The Kit-Bag* with the idea of 'Gothic horror' in stories, films, books and comics. The best way to do this is by devising a chart. List any Gothic titles you can think of along the top and tick the boxes which correspond with the right elements.

Be sure to leave a few blank rows and columns of boxes that can be filled in later as you discover more.

- Collect any words or phrases that keep cropping up in your discussion – 'graveyards', 'the moon', 'skulls' – and add them to the Gothic Collage that has been created by the class.

▼ Elements	The Kit-Bag	Film	TV	Comic	
Person alone	✔				
Darkness	✔				
Unknown noises	✔				

DESCENDING INTO HORROR

People are fascinated by fear. They have written and read about it for hundreds of years. As you read the rest of the extracts in this unit, look out for:

- Common elements

- The techniques used by the writers to create fear

- Underlying themes such as darkness, 'power'...what else?

DRACULA

One of the most famous Gothic horror stories is *Dracula*, written by Bram Stoker and published in 1897. Much of the story is told by the young hero, Jonathan Harker, in a journal he uses to record his experiences. In this extract, he is suspicious of the Count and is searching for his secret...

'At one corner of the room was a heavy door. I tried it, for, since I could not find the key of the room or the key of the outer door, which was the main object of my search, I must make further examination, or all my efforts would be in vain. It was open, and led through a stone passage to a circular stairway, which went steeply down. I descended, minding carefully where I went, for the stairs were dark, being only lit by loopholes in the heavy masonry. At the bottom there was a dark, tunnel-like passage, through which came a deathly, sickly odour, the odour of old earth newly turned. As I went through the passage the smell grew closer and heavier.

At last I pulled open a heavy door which stood ajar, and found myself in an old, ruined chapel, which had evidently been used as a graveyard. The roof was broken, and in two places were steps leading to vaults, but the ground had recently been dug over, and the earth placed in great wooden boxes, manifestly those which had been brought by the Slovaks. There was nobody about, and I made search for any further outlet, but there was none. Then I went over every inch of the ground, so as not to lose a chance. I went down even into the vaults, where the dim light struggled, although to do so was a dread to my very soul. Into two of these I went, but saw nothing except fragments of old coffins and piles of dust; in the third, however, I made a discovery.

There, in one of the great boxes, of which there were fifty in all, on a pile of newly dug earth, lay the Count! He was either dead or asleep, I could not say which – for the eyes were open and stony, but without the glassiness of death – and the cheeks had the warmth of life through all their pallor, and the lips were as red as ever. But there was no sign of movement, no pulse, no breath, no beating of the heart. I bent over him, and tried to find any sign of life, but in vain. He could not have lain there long, for the earthy smell would have passed away in a few hours. By the side of the box was its cover, pierced with holes here and there. I thought he might have the keys on him, but when I went to search I saw the dead eyes, and in them, dead though they were, such a look of hate, though unconscious of me or my presence, that I fled from the place, and leaving the Count's room by the window, crawled again up the castle wall. Regaining my own chamber, I threw myself panting upon the bed and tried to think…'

A GOTHIC ATMOSPHERE

- Working by yourself, imagine that this extract is being filmed. You are the director and you want to give instructions to the camera crew about how to capture the right atmosphere. Complete the list below:

Shot	Visual Image	Sound Track
1	View down the dark tunnel-like passage	Dripping water
2	The heavy door at the end of the passage	A hand scrabbling to open the door
3	The scene through the open door of the ruined chapel	A brief but sudden and loud noise like a high pitched note on a violin

There has recently been a huge increase in the number of horror books published for teenagers. There are Gothic elements in many of these stories…

THE ATTIC

by T S Rae

Tessa was alone, back in the cold, dark stairwell. She didn't know how she had gotten there. Spinning around frantically, she searched for a door to bang on, but there wasn't one. All there was were cold, gray cinder-block walls, an icy metal rail, and stairs that led nowhere.

Tessa refused to take the step into blackness. If there wasn't a door on this landing, she'd go up and find one. She started climbing the stairs. She knew she'd come to the next landing soon.

But the stairs went up and up and up...

After a while Tessa had to stop climbing and catch her breath. Her legs were exhausted. She reached for the rail for support. Oddly, it had changed from metal to wood, like the banister that led to the attic. And the walls were no longer cinder block. They were covered with yellow, flowery wallpaper.

Tessa took another breath, trying to decide what to do. Below her the steps disappeared into darkness. Above her the steps seemed to go up and up endlessly.

Then Tessa heard it – that faint, scratchy sound. It seemed to be coming from below. She didn't know what was making the noise, but she wasn't going to wait around to find out.

She started climbing the stairs again, but she wasn't getting anywhere.

The stairs had started to move. It was like trying to climb up a down escalator. . . . No matter how fast she climbed, she stayed in the same place.

And the scratching sound was growing louder.

Tessa was no longer walking up the stairs. Now she was running.

The sound grew louder still.

It didn't make sense. How could it be going up the stairs faster than she? Tessa climbed faster. . . as fast as she could. She wouldn't look behind, wouldn't look at whatever was making that noise.

The scratching noise was getting even louder.

Don't look! Don't look!

MORE GOTHIC ELEMENTS

- Working with a partner, go back to the chart you created when you were trying to see elements of Gothic horror in *The Kit-Bag*.

  You were asked to leave some columns blank. Now add *Dracula* and *The Attic* and fill in the boxes.

▼ Elements	The Kit-Bag	Film	TV	Comic	Dracula	The Attic
Person alone	✔				✔	✔
Darkness	✔				✔	✔
Unknown noises	✔					✔

- Looking at the last two extracts from *Dracula* and *The Attic*, which one seems to you to be the most successful? What do you think are the particular strengths of each piece? Which words and phrases would you single out to illustrate the different ways in which each extract is written?

- As a class, add your observations to the Gothic Collage. You should devise your own way of displaying the work that you have done, but you might:

  ▶ design book covers for each story, bringing out the Gothic elements in each

  or

  ▶ write out – and perhaps illustrate – key quotations from the stories, which bring out their Gothic qualities

  or

  ▶ display the two extracts side-by-side, with your comparisons to accompany them.

SPOTLIGHT ON FEAR

You have now studied a short story and two extracts from horror stories, identifying common elements and styles.

- Working by yourself, create your own piece of writing that builds tension and fear in a similar way. The challenge is to do this in no more than two or three paragraphs, without revealing exactly what it is that is so terrifying.

FACE TO FACE

Writers of horror often bring the reader face to face with the truly horrible. In his story *The Haunted Hotel,* Wilkie Collins finally describes a ghastly apparition:

By the yellow candle-light she saw the head distinctly, hovering in mid-air above her. She looked at it steadfastly, spell-bound by the terror that held her.

The flesh of the face was gone. The shrivelled skin was darkened in hue, like the skin of an Egyptian mummy – except at the neck. There it was of a lighter colour; there it showed spots and splashes of the hue of that brown spot on the ceiling, which the child's fanciful terror had distorted into the likeness of a spot of blood. The remains of a discoloured moustache and whiskers, hanging over the upper lip, and over the hollows where the cheeks had once been, made the head just recognisable as the head of a man. Over all the features death and time had done their obliterating work. The eyelids were closed. The hair on the skull, discoloured like the hair on the face, had been burnt away in places. The bluish lips, parted in a fixed grin, showed the double row of teeth. By slow degrees the hovering head (perfectly still when she first saw it) began to descend towards Agnes as she lay beneath.

In *Jane Eyre* by Charlotte Brontë, Jane has to stay guarding an horrifically injured man close to a room that houses his attacker:

I must watch this ghastly countenance – these blue, still lips forbidden to unclose – these eyes now shut, now opening, now wandering through the room, now fixing on me, and ever glazed with the dullness of horror. I must dip my hand again and again in the basin of blood and water, and wipe away the trickling gore. I must see the light of the unsnuffed candle wane on my employment; the shadows darken on the wrought, antique tapestry round me, and grow black under the hangings of the vast old bed, and quiver strangely over the doors of a great cabinet opposite...

... Amidst all this, I had to listen as well as watch; to listen for the movements of the wild beast or fiend in yonder side-den. But since Mr Rochester's visit it seemed spell bound: all the night I heard but three sounds at three long intervals – a sharp creak, a momentary renewal of the snarling canine noise, and a deep human groan.

THE TRULY HORRIBLE

- Working with a partner, discuss how 'the truly horrible' is described in these extracts. Choose a word, phrase or sentence that is important in creating the effect the writer wants. Comment on the effect of the words and sentence structure. How many members of the class chose the same phrase?

Detailed descriptions of blood and gore are not, however, always essential in a horror story. *The Kit-Bag* hints at the ghoulish nature of the crime committed by John Turk, but the full horror of the story lies in imagining what might lie in store for Johnson.

- Discuss which approach you find more effective: vividly gory description or a story that depends more upon the reader's imagination.

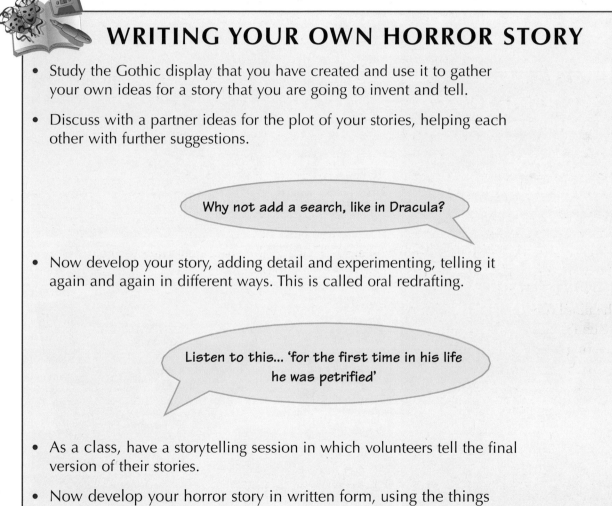

WRITING YOUR OWN HORROR STORY

- Study the Gothic display that you have created and use it to gather your own ideas for a story that you are going to invent and tell.

- Discuss with a partner ideas for the plot of your stories, helping each other with further suggestions.

> Why not add a search, like in Dracula?

- Now develop your story, adding detail and experimenting, telling it again and again in different ways. This is called oral redrafting.

> Listen to this... 'for the first time in his life he was petrified'

- As a class, have a storytelling session in which volunteers tell the final version of their stories.

- Now develop your horror story in written form, using the things you have learnt so far in this unit.

Puffin Book Club

POST New Year 1996

SEETHING INSIDE

▲ **Gothic Romance -** A brand new series
▲ **The latest Puffin Post magazine**
▲ **The Bewitching of Alison Allbright**
▲ **Babe** Film Tie-ins

FREE
POSTCARD WITH EVERY BOOK

COLLECT THE SERIES!

NEW

1. ADVENTURES OF GOLDHAWK MUDWORM SWAMP
Ian Livingstone
The third of the new full-colour First Fighting Fantasies - are you daring enough to take up the challenge? You must venture into the sulphurous mudworm swamps of Northern Karazan to find a badly needed antidote, and the Marsh Zombies and Swamp Riders are only two of the enemies you must face.
64pages FULL COLOUR

CLUB PRICE

£3.99 £3.80

FREE COMPETITION INSIDE

NEW

The Wacky World of Wesley Baker
GENE KEMP

3. THE WACKY WORLD OF WESLEY BAKER
Gene Kemp
Misplaced in a family of fitness freaks, Wesley's dad puts him on an intensive bodybuilding course for sports day, where he is also pursued by the gruesome Agnes Potter! And is there really a dragon dwelling under the hall platform or has Wesley finally cracked!
160pages

£3.99

2. SIT DOWN MUM, THERE'S SOMETHING I'VE GOT TO TELL YOU
Moya Simons
Hatty sees the perfect opportunity for a spot of match-making for her lonely Mum in the personal column of the local paper and begins a long correspondence (posing as her mum) with Morris the would-be poet. But what will happen when the truth comes out?
132pages

NEW

£3.50

CLUB PRICE

GILLIAN CROSS
THE DEMON HEADMASTER AND THE PRIME MINISTER'S BRAIN
Now a BBC series

THE LITTLE BOOK *or NEW YEAR'S RESOLUTIONS
SHOO RAYNER

CLUB PRICE

5. THE LITTLE BOOK OF NEW YEAR'S RESOLUTIONS
Shoo Rayner
Here's one resolution that shouldn't be hard to keep - read this book and have lots of laughs!
64pages

£2.50 £1.99

4. THE DEMON HEADMASTER AND THE PRIME MINISTER'S BRAIN
Gillian Cross
He's wicked, he's evil and he plans to take over the country. Only Dinah and the other members of SPLAT can hope to save the nation from the deadly grip of their Demon Headmaster. Now a stunning BBC TV series.
304pages

£4.99 £4.50

THE GOTHIC BOOK CLUB

The final task in this unit is to use all that you have learned to create your own Book Club on a Gothic theme – the GOTHIC BOOK CLUB.

- Look carefully at the example on the opposite page of the 'Puffin Book Club'. It includes advertisements, special offers, free gifts, and brief reviews. What would you want to include in the Gothic Book Club?

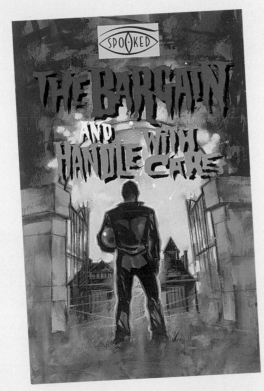

- Which books will you choose? You may need to do some further reading in order to find other stories and novels that have elements of the Gothic. Try a modern Gothic tale such as *The Stories of Muncaster Cathedral* by Robert Westall. You might also want to invent some titles of your own.

- Design and write your own version of the Gothic Book Club News Sheet.

WHAT NEXT?

In this unit you have examined what is meant by 'the Gothic' through photographs and illustrations as well as a wide range of Gothic horror writing. You have built up a comprehensive picture of Gothic elements in literature, producing a Gothic collage and a Gothic story of your own making.

This unit has also focused on the way writers influence the feelings of their characters by manipulating nature: darkness, rain, cold, the workings of the human body. As you read the next unit, bear in mind your knowledge of 'the Gothic' and see if you can find any links with Shakespeare's own intense and highly–charged world.

When you move on to more advanced work next year, you will find yourself studying books more closely and you will find that it helps you to know about the type, or 'genre', of book you are reading as well as the individual title. What other genres besides Gothic horror can you think of?

At the end of the last unit, you were asked to devise a publicity campaign to promote reading in the school. One possible approach is to try to make recommendations for further reading based on genres that are already well known and liked. An example might be science fiction, since you can be fairly confident that somebody who likes Terry Pratchett will also enjoy reading *Red Dwarf*. What would you suggest they try next - Star Wars? Isaac Asimov? John Wyndham?

• Try producing some reading trails that you could display in order to help 11-14 year olds who are wondering what to read next. Here is an example:

Adventure

If you have read	Enid Blyton's *The Castle of Adventure*
You might enjoy	Arthur Ransome's *Pigeon Post*
Followed by	Brian Jacques' *Redwall*
Before trying	Joan Aiken's *The Wolves of Willoughby Chase*

Macbeth

The aim of this unit is to become familiar with one of Shakespeare's plays by studying it in detail and examining a number of key characters and themes. You will be asked to interpret parts of the play and understand why characters behave as they do. As you work through this unit, you will develop your skills as:

SPEAKERS AND LISTENERS

by acting out scenes and taking part in improvisations
by discussing issues, meanings, events and characters

READERS

by studying key scenes
by becoming more familiar with Shakespeare's use of language

WRITERS

by writing in role as a key character
by practising examination style questions

Now read on to find out how Macbeth changes from being a brave and noble warrior to a cruel and ruthless tyrant…

A DREADFUL DILEMMA!

Imagine this – you want something very badly. You could just wait and see what happens … perhaps somebody might even give this thing to you without your having to do anything for it? This is your first option. There is a second option however … you could just take this thing that you want so badly but this would involve doing something which you know is terribly wrong. You feel impatient and you are easily tempted. Somebody close to you is trying to persuade you to choose the second option.

• Work in pairs to act out the situation described above. Make up a dilemma. Improvise the conversation which might take place. Present your conversation to the class.

> **Dilemma** – A situation in which somebody has to make a difficult choice between two unpleasant courses of action.
>
> **Improvise** – Act out a situation without a script. It may change slightly each time you practise it.

In the play, Macbeth himself is faced with a dilemma and one of the key moments in the play is when his wife tries to persuade him to do the wrong thing.

CLUES IN THE LANGUAGE

The following lines are taken from key moments in the play.
Read them through to yourself.

'Stars, hide your fires!
Let not light see my black and deep desires!'

'We will proceed no further in this business.'

'look like the innocent flower
But be the serpent under't.'

'The devil himself could not pronounce a title
More hateful to mine ear.'

'My hands are of your colour, but I shame
To wear a heart so white.'

'Thou canst not say I did it: never shake
Thy gory locks at me.'

'Out, damned spot! out, I say!'

'A little water clears us of this deed;'

'Is this a dagger which I see before me,
The handle toward my hand?'

Work with a partner. What impressions do you get from these lines about the events of the play? For each quotation, decide what kind of person might say it and why. What might the words mean?

Choose three quotations. Practise speaking each of your quotations aloud.

- Try speaking each one in different ways – for example, angrily, nervously, confidently.

- With your partner, discuss how the way you speak each quotation can change your interpretation of it.

Shakespeare's language is very rich, and laden with different meanings.

THE PLAY BEGINS

In Shakespeare's time, people were very superstitious. They believed in witches. Thousands of women were accused of being witches and were put to death, either by burning, hanging or drowning. In reality, these were innocent women who were falsely accused because people were so superstitious and afraid.

People believed that witches could:

- communicate with the Devil
- see into the future
- cast spells that would make people ill or even kill them
- cause bad weather such as storms or fog, and turn day into night
- become invisible
- fly through the air.

The King of England, James I, believed that a group of witches had tried to drown him and his wife. He even wrote a book about witches called 'Demonology'.

START READING

Now read the first scene in the play, Act 1 Scene 1. It begins with the three witches meeting on a deserted moor.

What advantages would Shakespeare have seen in opening the play with a scene about witches?

Shakespeare's theatre, The Globe, was open to the sun and rain. The plays were performed in the day time. There was no scenery and few props. It would be difficult to create a spooky mood for this scene. How do you think they managed this?

READ ON

Now read or watch the play up to the end of Act 1.

HELP

HOW THE PLAY IS ORGANISED

Like all of Shakespeare's plays, *Macbeth* is divided into five acts. Each act is divided into a number of scenes. The act and scene numbers are usually printed at the top of each page. You may also find line numbers printed down the side of your text. This is to help you find your way around the play and to make it easier for you to refer to a quotation, for example:

'Fair is foul and foul is fair' is from Act 1, Scene 1, line 11; or I.i.11.

ACT 1

What happens?

Scene 1
- The witches meet and plan their encounter with Macbeth.

Scene 2
- King Duncan wins an important battle against Norway.
- The Thane of Cawdor has been treacherous.
- Macbeth and Banquo have fought bravely for Duncan.
- Duncan decides to execute the Thane of Cawdor and to give his title to Macbeth.

Scene 3
- The witches meet Macbeth and Banquo on their way back from the battlefield.
- They tell Macbeth that he will be Thane of Cawdor and then King.
- They tell Banquo that his sons will be kings.
- Ross tells Macbeth that Duncan has rewarded him with the title Thane of Cawdor.
- Macbeth is unsettled by this news – the first prophecy has already come true!

Scene 4
- Duncan names his son Malcolm as his successor. Macbeth is disappointed.

Scene 5
- Lady Macbeth receives a letter from her husband. She is determined that he should become king.
- Macbeth arrives home and she tells him her plan.

Scene 6
- Duncan arrives to spend the night at Macbeth's castle.

Scene 7
- Macbeth has doubts about the murder but Lady Macbeth convinces him that he must murder Duncan.

FOCUS ON: WHO'S WHO

•Lady Macbeth• •Macduff and family• •Duncan• •Malcolm• •Donalbain• •Banquo•

•Macbeth• •Fleance•

Here is a picture of the main characters.

For each character write down:
• their job or their relationship with other characters
• three things they do in Act 1
• your impressions so far of the type of character he or she seems to be.

FOCUS ON: THE WITCHES

Read Act 1 Scene 3, lines 38–78 (from 'So foul and fair a day I have not seen' to 'Witches vanish') in which Macbeth and Banquo meet the witches.

Find the lines where:
• Macbeth seems startled by the witches' prophecies
• Banquo asks the witches to predict his future
• Macbeth challenges what the witches have told him.

Now read on to the end of the scene.

Find the lines where:
• Banquo is shocked and realises that there may be some truth in what the witches have said

• Macbeth begins to think about the second prophecy
• Banquo warns Macbeth that the witches may mean to harm them
• Macbeth suggests to Banquo that they should speak privately about what has happened.

Macbeth is keen to be King. Find two things that might please him about the prophecies, and two things that might worry him about them.

FOCUS ON: MACBETH'S DILEMMA

Soliloquy – A speech in a play which is not spoken to another character on the stage. The character speaking the words seems to be thinking his or her thoughts aloud.

Aside – A speech which is spoken directly to the audience rather than to another character on stage.

Read the soliloquy in Act 1 Scene 7 beginning 'If it were done when 'tis done', in which Macbeth has doubts about the murder of Duncan.

- Find five reasons why Macbeth tells himself he should not murder Duncan.
- Find the one reason why Macbeth is still likely to murder Duncan.

Now read on to the end of the scene. Lady Macbeth finds her husband and tries to persuade him to commit the murder, be he has doubts.

- List the reasons Macbeth gives to his wife not to do the murder.
- Study her answers and list all the ways she tries to persuade him to do it.

Lady Macbeth has no real arguments on her side. Clearly it would be wrong to murder Duncan. Instead, she uses persuasion to convince her husband that he should carry out the murder.

Complete the speech bubbles, using your own words to present Macbeth's arguments against the murder and some of Lady Macbeth's persuasive tactics.

Now read or watch to the end of Act 2.

ACT 2
What happens?

Scene 1
- It is the night of the murder. Macbeth speaks with Banquo and denies ever thinking about the witches. He sees an imaginary dagger which seems to be pointing towards Duncan's room.

Scene 2
- Macbeth murders Duncan.
- Lady Macbeth takes the daggers back to the scene of the crime.
- There is knocking at the castle door.

Scene 3
- The Porter opens the gate to Macduff.
- The murder is discovered.
- Malcolm and Donalbain flee to England and to Ireland.

Scene 4
- Strange things happen in the natural world.
- Macbeth has gone to be crowned King.
- Macduff decides not to attend the coronation.

FOCUS ON: THE NIGHT OF THE MURDER – TENSION AND SUSPENSE

As Lady Macbeth waits for her husband to murder Duncan, the scene is charged with an electric tension. So how does Shakespeare fill the scene with tension?

Re-read Act 2 Scene 2. How does Shakespeare create such a tense atmosphere in this scene?

Make notes on:
- the time
- the place
- the sounds
- the feelings of the characters
- the length of sentences
- the words and phrases that are used.

FOCUS ON MACBETH AND LADY MACBETH

Lady Macbeth seems to be strong and in control of the situation because:

- She has planned the murder
- She takes the bloodstained daggers back to the scene of the crime and smears the guards with blood
- She calms her husband and makes him wash the blood from his hands.

What evidence is there, however, that she is not as strong as she seems? Find clues in this scene and any from earlier in the play.

Macbeth, on the other hand, seems to depend on his wife for support. He seems to lose confidence and allows Lady Macbeth to take control. Read the soliloquy in Act 2 Scene 1 which starts 'Is this a dagger which I see before me', and find places where:

- Macbeth is sure he can see a dagger
- Macbeth believes that the dagger is a figment of his imagination
- Macbeth knows why this is happening to him.

Soliloquies can reveal a great deal about a character's true thoughts and feelings. What does Macbeth reveal about his state of mind in this soliloquy?

Now close your copy of the play and read the final part of the soliloquy in Act 2 Scene 1 below. Some words have been left out. With your partner, discuss which words would best fit each gap. You will find the words at the end of the soliloquy.

'Thou sure and _____ earth,
Hear not my steps, which way they walk, for fear
Thy very _____ prate of my whereabout,
And take the present _____ from the time,
Which now suits with it. Whiles I _____, he lives:
Words to the _____ of deeds too cold breath gives.
(*A bell rings*)
I go, and it is done; the bell _____ me.
Hear it not, Duncan; for it is a knell
That _____ thee to heaven, or to _____ .'

invites	firm-set
horror	summons
hell	threat
stones	heat

HELP

Prate – tell

- Look back at the soliloquy in your play to find Shakespeare's own words. Why has he chosen these words and not others that could have been used? What is the dramatic effect of this?

- Who rings the bell at the end of Macbeth's soliloquy and how do you know?

FOCUS ON: HUMOUR – THE PORTER

After the tension and suspense of Duncan's murder, and before the horror of the discovery of the murder, Shakespeare introduces the audience to the Porter. The Porter has been woken up by Macduff's knocking; he is none too pleased because he had a lot to drink the night before. He imagines he is the porter at the gate of Hell.

Read again Act 2 Scene 3, from the beginning of the scene to line 42.

- With a partner, practise acting out the Porter's first speech.
- Read it aloud, trying out different accents each time.
- Try pacing the room, changing direction each time you reach a punctuation mark.
- The Porter is quite rude and bawdy at times. Can you find an example of something he says which would have made the audience laugh?
- Why do you think Shakespeare might have wanted the audience to laugh at this point in the play?

Now read on or watch to the end of Act 3.

ACT 3
What happens?

Scene 1
- Macbeth is now King but Banquo is suspicious of him.
- Macbeth invites Banquo to a great feast.
- Macbeth hires murderers to kill Banquo and his son Fleance.

Scene 2
- Macbeth does not tell his wife his plans for Banquo.

Scene 3
- Banquo is murdered – Fleance escapes.

Scene 4
- The banquet scene. Macbeth sees the ghost of Banquo.
- The guests are shocked at Macbeth's strange behaviour.
- Macduff has offended Macbeth by not attending his feast.
- Macbeth plans to visit the witches.

Scene 5
- The witches meet.

Scene 6
- The people of Scotland are now suspicious of Macbeth.

FOCUS ON: BANQUO

- Discuss what you already know about Banquo, then read the following speeches, all spoken by Banquo:

To Macbeth on seeing the witches for the first time:

'Good sir, why do you start; and seem to fear
Things that do sound so fair? I' the name of truth,
Are ye fantastical, or that indeed
Which outwardly ye show?
(I.iii)

To the witches on first meeting:

My noble partner
You greet with present grace and great prediction
Of noble having and of royal hope,
That he seems rapt withal: to me you speak not.
If you can look into the seeds of time,
And say which grain will grow and which will not,
Speak then to me, who neither beg nor fear
Your favours nor your hate.'
(I.iii)

To Macbeth just after Duncan's dead body has been found:

'Look to the lady:
And when we have our naked frailties hid,
That suffer in exposure, let us meet,
And question this most bloody piece of work,
To know it further. Fears and scruples shake us:
In the great hand of God I stand; and thence
Against the undivulged pretence I fight
Of treasonous malice.'
(II.iii)

Banquo

To himself shortly before Macbeth murders him:

'Thou hast it now: king, Cawdor, Glamis, all,
As the weird women promised; and, I fear,
Thou play'dst most foully for 't; yet it was said
It should not stand in thy posterity,
But that myself should be the root and father
Of many kings. If there come truth from them–
As upon thee, Macbeth, their speeches shine–
Why, by the verities on thee made good,
May they not be my oracles as well,
And set me up in hope?'
(III.i)

What do you learn about Banquo's character from each of these speeches?

In what ways is he different from Macbeth? Consider:
- his reaction to the witches
- his reaction to Duncan's murder
- his attitude towards Macbeth.

FOCUS ON: THE BANQUET SCENE

After Macbeth has had Banquo murdered, he thinks his position will be safer. However, Banquo's son Fleance has escaped and may still become a king as the witches promised. The ghost of Banquo appears at Macbeth's banquet.

- What do we learn about Macbeth's state of mind at this point in the play?
- How do the guests react to Macbeth's strange behaviour?
- How does Lady Macbeth deal with the situation?

Look at the picture below.
- We know what the characters actually say during this scene but what might they be thinking? Work with a partner to complete the thought bubbles.

Macbeth:
Quit my sight! Let the earth hide thee!
Thy bones are marrowless, thy blood is cold;
Thou hast no speculation in those eyes
Which thou dost glare with

Lady Macbeth:
Sit, worthy friends: my lord is often thus,
And hath been from his youth: pray you, keep seat;
The fit is momentary

Ross:
Gentleman, rise his highness is not well

Lennox:
Good-night; and better health
Attend his majesty!

FOCUS ON: THE DIRECTION OF THE PLOT

Discuss what the rest of the play might be about.
- What needs to be resolved?
- How could things get better?
- How could things get worse?

In Shakespeare's five-act structure, the fourth act often sees matters get even more complicated and intense. What more could happen in *Macbeth* to make matters worse?

At the end of Act 3, it is clear that all is not well with Macbeth. Macduff has snubbed his invitation to the banquet and we discover that Macbeth feels so insecure, he keeps a spy in all the thanes' houses. He decides to visit the witches.

Work in groups to discuss the following:
- what might happen when Macbeth visits the witches?
- what Macduff might do and why?
- what might happen to Lady Macbeth?

Now read on or watch to the end of Act 4.

ACT 4
What happens?

Scene 1
- Macbeth visits the witches; he wants more information. They show him three apparitions, and make three more prophecies.
- Macbeth is told that Macduff has fled to England.
- Macbeth plans to have Macduff's family murdered.

Scene 2
- Macduff's family is murdered.

Scene 3
- The scene changes to England. Macduff and Malcolm plan to raise an army and march on Scotland.
- Macduff receives news of his family.

FOCUS ON: THE APPARITIONS

Macbeth decides that he would rather hear the answers to his questions from the witches' masters than from the witches themselves. He is associating himself with the deepest and darkest forces of evil.

- What is the first apparition?
- What does it tell Macbeth?

- What is the second apparition?
- What does it tell Macbeth?

- What is the third apparition?
- What does it tell Macbeth?

- What final piece of information does Macbeth want to know?
- What is he shown and what does it mean?

As a result of his second encounter with the witches, Macbeth feels that he cannot be beaten. Could he be wrong? Think of ways in which the apparitions could deceive him.

FOCUS ON: MACDUFF

We can learn about a character by:

- what they say
- what they do
- what others say about them
- comparing them to others.

Macduff

What do we learn about Macduff? With a partner, discuss the following:

- his reaction to Duncan's murder
- his attitude to Macbeth's coronation
- his attitude towards Macbeth's invitation to the banquet
- his fleeing to England
- his meeting with Malcolm
- his reaction to the news of the slaughter of his family
- his attitude to Macbeth.

Act 4 Scene 3, in which Macduff meets Malcolm in England, is a long scene, which is often edited when the play is produced on stage. Work in a group to edit the scene to approximately 60 lines – one quarter of its original length. The completed version should make sense and you should end up with correct punctuation.

Perform your edited version to the rest of the class.

HELP

Discuss which you think are the most important things which are said or done in this scene, for example:

- Malcolm tests Macduff to make sure he is honest

- Macduff receives news of his family.

When you have selected the lines you wish to include, write out your edited scene, linking them together so that they make sense.

Now read on or watch to the end of Act 5.

ACT 5
What happens?

Scene 1
- Lady Macbeth sleepwalks. Her guilt is apparent.

Scene 2
- The Scottish rebels plan to join forces with the English army at Birnam.

Scene 3
- Macbeth receives news of the approaching English army.
- Lady Macbeth is ill.

Scene 4
- The English soldiers cut down branches in Birnam Wood for camouflage.

Scene 5
- Lady Macbeth dies.
- Macbeth receives news of the 'moving wood'.
- Macbeth begins to realise that he has been tricked by the witches.

Scene 6
- Macduff and Malcolm approach Macbeth's castle.

Scene 7
- Macbeth kills Young Siward.
- Macduff tells Macbeth he was born by Caesarean birth. He kills Macbeth.
- Malcolm is crowned King of Scotland.

FOCUS ON: LADY MACBETH

Re-read Act 5 Scene 1 in which Lady Macbeth is seen sleepwalking by the Doctor and her Gentlewoman.

Find five things which she says or does whilst sleepwalking which refer to things which have happened earlier in the play.

Why do you think Lady Macbeth, rather than Macbeth, has gone mad? Look for clues earlier in the play, for example:

- the scene in which she receives the letter from her husband
- the scene in which she persuades Macbeth to murder Duncan
- the scene immediately after the murder of Duncan in which she takes the daggers back to the murder scene.

With a partner, discuss the following:
- Why does Lady Macbeth urge her husband to kill Duncan?
- How well does Lady Macbeth really understand her husband?
- Does she behave in a way which is natural to her?
- Why doesn't she murder Duncan herself?
- Why does Macbeth gradually begin to leave her out of his plans?
- Why has she gone mad?

Look back through the play to find the last time the audience see Lady Macbeth before the sleepwalking scene. Why do you think Shakespeare left her out of the play for such a long time?

Ellen Terry as Lady Macbeth, 1889, by John Singer Sargent

FOCUS ON: MACBETH

Macbeth

All of the words below describe Macbeth at different times in the play. For each word, give an example of something he says or does in the play which confirms it.

Word	Evidence
ambitious	
gullible	
brutal	
brave	
loyal	
suspicious	
ruthless	
guilty	
treacherous	
greedy	
stressed	
heroic	
indecisive	
weak	
depressed	

FOCUS ON: SPEAKING AND LISTENING – MACBETH ON TRIAL

Imagine that Macbeth is not killed but captured at the end of the play. Organise a courtroom scene in which you put him on trial. You will need to work in groups of about ten. You will need:

- a judge
- a prosecution lawyer
- a defence lawyer
- Macbeth
- witnesses, for example, Macduff, Malcolm, the Gentlewoman, the Porter.

The prosecution and the defence will consider what questions to ask and which witnesses to call. Consider:

- whether Macbeth is a brave, loyal soldier at the beginning of the play or a brutal, ruthless mercenary
- whether he thinks of murdering Duncan before his wife suggests it
- why he allows his wife to persuade him to commit murder if he doesn't want to do it
- his treatment of Banquo
- his hallucinations – the ghost and the dagger
- the brutal killings of the guards and Macduff's family
- his treatment of his wife later on in the play.

In the end, everyone else in the class can vote guilty or not guilty.

HELP

Ten Top Tips

1 Research your character – you will be speaking in role.
2 Plan what you want to say.
3 Do not write your words out in full – you will be tempted to read aloud from them.
4 Make notes/keywords on cards – you may need to prompt yourself.
5 Rehearse your part at home – in front of a mirror if necessary!
6 Make sure your group has time to practise together – what you say will depend on others' contributions as well.
7 Speak clearly.
8 Don't rush your words.
9 Establish eye contact with the person you are speaking to.
10 Remember to listen to others and to respond to what they say.

FOCUS ON: *MACBETH* AS A TRAGEDY

Shakespeare wrote plays which can be divided loosely into three categories:

- histories
- comedies
- tragedies.

There are five main ingredients in Shakespeare's tragedies:

1 The play is concerned with the main male character – the hero.
2 The hero is of noble birth.
3 The hero has a weakness of character (sometimes called a fatal flaw).

4 The hero's weakness of character, as well as events outside his control, contribute to his downfall.
5 The hero dies at the end of the play.

Check each ingredient to see whether you agree that *Macbeth* is a tragedy.

FOCUS ON: THEMES

- Here are some of the other main themes of the play. Copy the plan onto a separate piece of paper and add any more you can think of.

- Around each theme, gather examples of events, words and characters linked to each theme.

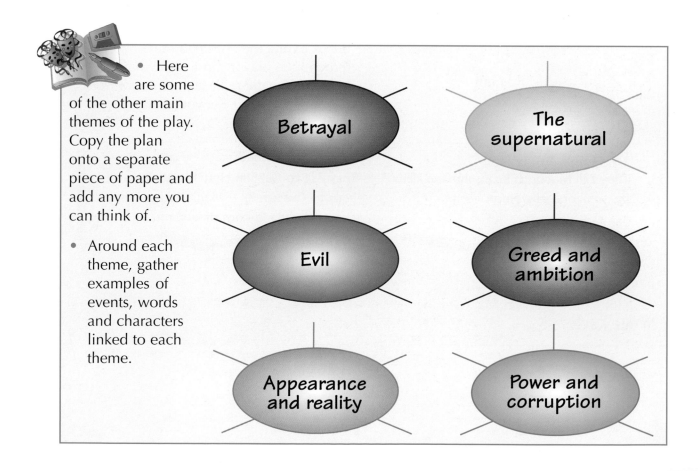

Betrayal

The supernatural

Evil

Greed and ambition

Appearance and reality

Power and corruption

FOCUS ON: A THEME – APPEARANCE AND REALITY

The play dwells on the difference between the way things look and the way they really are. For example:

- Lady Macbeth seems like a charming hostess but in reality she is planning Duncan's murder.

- By running away, Malcolm and Donalbain seem guilty but in reality they are innocent.

- The witches seem to be helping Macbeth but in reality they are deliberately misleading him.

Can you think of other examples? Jot them down.

Shakespeare's *language* also echoes this theme. For example:

'Fair is foul and foul is fair'
(I.i)

'Good sir, why do you start, and seem to fear
Things that do sound so fair?'
(I.iii)

'False face must hide what the false heart doth know.'
(I.vii)

'look like the innocent flower
But be the serpent under 't.'
(I.v)

'make our faces vizards to our hearts,
Disguising what they are.'
(III.ii)

- Who speaks each line and to whom? What are they saying about appearance and reality?

- The witches also seem to tell the truth but in reality they mislead Macbeth. Look through the play again to see what the witches actually tell Macbeth. How do they mislead him? Set your findings out in a chart like this:

What they say	How they mislead
They tell Macbeth he cannot be killed by someone of woman born.	They fail to tell him that Macduff was born by Caesarean – Macbeth assumes that everyone is born of woman.

- Why do you think the witches deliberately mislead Macbeth in this way?

FOCUS ON: SHAKESPEARE'S VERSE

As you read the play, you may have noticed that some speeches are written in poetry whilst others are written in prose.

Look at Malcolm's final speech at the end of the play.

'We shall not spend a large expense of time
Before we reckon with your several loves …'

Here, Shakespeare is writing in poetry. He is using **blank verse**.
   Blank verse:
* does not rhyme
* has ten syllables in each line
* uses an iambic rhythm (the rhythm falls on every second syllable: soft-hard, soft-hard, etc).

   x   /   x   /   x   /   x   /   x   /
We shall not spend a large expanse of time

Now look at the Porter's speech at the beginning of Act 2 Scene 3.

'Here's a knocking, indeed! If a man were porter of hell-gate, he should have old turning the key.'

Here, Shakespeare is writing in **prose**.
   Prose:
* is organised into paragraphs
* is not regulated by line length
* is closer to ordinary speech.

Shakespeare often uses prose for the comic scenes or the 'low life' characters.

Look for the following speeches and:
* work out if they are in blank verse or prose; and
* if they are in verse, how many beats to a line.

1 The witches' spell.
2 Macbeth's soliloquy 'She should have died hereafter' when he hears his wife is dead.
3 The first time we hear Macbeth's voice.
4 The last time we hear Macbeth's voice.
5 The final lines of the play.

Focus on: Test Questions

If you have studied *Macbeth* for your Key Stage 3 tests in English, you will need to understand exactly what is required.

You may be asked to:

- write about a character or characters
- write about a theme
- write in role as if you are a character
- explain how Shakespeare creates excitement or humour, tension or suspense
- explain how you would direct a scene for the stage
- discuss how an audience might react to a particular scene.

You will need to be familiar with the whole play and have focused on one or two scenes from the play which have been set for study. Make sure that you know which scenes these are. Your teacher will be able to tell you.

HELP

When you write about 'Macbeth', you need to give evidence for your views. You can do this by summarising what is said, or by quoting. For example:

Macbeth finally realises that the witches have tricked him. He calls them 'juggling fiends', which shows that he thinks they are like devils, and are playing games with him.

And

Lady Macbeth says that they should be like a 'serpent' under an 'innocent flower'. This tells us that she is two-faced, wanting to appear natural on the surface, when she really is a snake, ready to bite and kill its victim with poison.

When you quote, remember that you should:

- only quote a few words at a time;

- put quotation marks round the words you have quoted;

- fit the quotation into your sentence structure.

- explain what your quotation (or summary) shows.

Remember also that you should use the present tense in writing about the play, because it exists now.

Try these two practice questions.

TEST QUESTION 1

Read Act 1 Scene 2. On their way back from battle, Macbeth and Banquo meet three witches.

Imagine you are going to direct this scene for a class performance. Explain how you want the student acting the part of Macbeth to show his reactions to the witches.

Before you begin to write you should decide what advice to give the student about:

- Macbeth's first reaction to the prophecies
- Macbeth's reaction when Ross tells him about the Thane of Cawdor
- how you want Macbeth to speak and behave during his speeches
- how you want Macbeth's reaction to contrast with Banquo's.

Read the task again before you begin to write your answer.

TEST QUESTION 2

Read Act 1 Scene 5. Lady Macbeth receives a letter from her husband.

Imagine you are Lady Macbeth. Write down your thoughts and feelings as you read the letter. You could begin:

'My husband! I've always known there were great things in store for us…'.

Before you begin to write you should decide what Lady Macbeth thinks and feels about:

- her husband's character
- her relationship with her husband
- her hopes and ambitions for her husband
- her hopes and ambitions for herself.

Remember to write as if you are Lady Macbeth.

Read the task again before you begin to write your answer.

WHAT NEXT?

• Watch the famous film version of *Macbeth* directed by Roman Polanski. Consider how close it is to your own interpretation of the play. How far do you agree with the decisions which have been made about casting, costume and set design?

• Write a review of a production of *Macbeth* which you may have watched, or of a filmed version of the play. Collect a range of theatre, TV or film reviews from newspapers and magazines. What are the 'rules' for this text-type?

• Look closely through the play for references to sleep, darkness and clothing. Choose one of these images and make a display for your classroom. Include as many quotations from the play as you can and illustrate the images. Write briefly about the importance of the image in the play.

• Read or watch another of Shakespeare's tragedies. There are recently made film versions of *Hamlet,* for example. Compare it to *Macbeth* and see if it contains the ingredients of a Shakespearian tragedy.

UNIT FOUR

Investigating Narrative Texts

The aim of this unit is to:
- focus on the narrative form
- prepare for the National Curriculum tests in English
- explore the National Curriculum marking schemes
- enable you to target specific areas of your work to improve.

As you work through this unit you will develop your skills as:

SPEAKERS AND LISTENERS

by working with a partner collaboratively and as a critical friend
by considering the effectiveness of language in a range of texts

READERS

by reading a variety of extracts and considering the conventions of each
by exploring meaning and understanding of texts

WRITERS

by developing your skills in writing a narrative in examination conditions
by peer and self marking of written comprehension
by identifying specific aspects to include in analysis and 'writing in the
    style of' exercises
by reading the work of other students and judging the content and
    standard using the marking criteria
by considering target audience as an essential feature in written material

Think about what you have already
written in the past. Do you write a diary?
Have you written a story as if you were
the main character? Turn the page to
learn about different narratives…

WRITING FROM A PERSONAL POINT OF VIEW

From our earliest years as writers we express our own thoughts, feelings, motives and desires. This personal perspective is a very effective style of writing. The obvious form of this is the **autobiography** – you have probably written at least part of your own autobiography at school. An autobiography is written about yourself and, largely, tells the factual details about your past.

In works of fiction it is also possible to write as if you are the person in the narrative. This is called **first person narrative**. Like the autobiography, this can be highly effective as it draws you in as a reader, it gives you details about a character's thoughts and feelings.

Both of these types of writing use **I**, as the character or person is writing about themselves.

Read the first extract below which is from an autobiography called *I Know Why the Caged Bird Sings* written by Maya Angelou. It is about her life in Stamps, Arkansas in the United States during the 1930s.

The second extract is by Elie Wiesel who was sent as a child to the Nazi death camps. 'Night' recalls his memories of that period.

Maya Angelou tells us about finding her mother, Elie Wiesel about losing his.

One Christmas we received gifts from our mother and father, who lived separately in a heaven called California, where we were told they could have all the oranges they could eat. And the sun shone all the time. I was sure that wasn't so. I couldn't believe that our mother would laugh and eat oranges in the sunshine without her children. Until that Christmas when we received the gifts I had been confident that they were both dead. I could cry anytime I wanted picturing my mother (I didn't quite know what she looked like) lying in her coffin. Her hair, which was black, was spread out on a tiny little white pillow and her body was covered with a sheet. The face was brown like a big O, and since I couldn't fill in the features I printed MOTHER across the O, and tears would fall down my cheeks like warm milk.

The came that terrible Christmas with its awful presents when our father, with the vanity I was to find typical, sent his photograph. My gift from my Mother was a tea set – a teapot, four cups and saucers and tiny spoons – and a doll with blue eyes and rosy cheeks and yellow hair painted on her head. I didn't know what Bailey received, but after I opened my boxes I went out to the backyard behind the chinaberry tree. The day was cold and the air was clear as water. Frost was still on the bench but I sat down and cried. I looked up and Bailey was coming from the outhouse, wiping his eyes. He had been crying too. I didn't know if he had also told himself they were dead and had been rudely awakened to the truth or whether he was just feeling lonely. The gifts opened the door to questions that neither of us wanted to ask. Why did they send us away? And What did we do so wrong? So Wrong? Why, at three and four, did we have tags put on our arms to be sent by train alone from Long Beach, California, to Stamps, Arkansas, with only the porter to look after us? (Besides, he got off in Arizona.)

The cherished objects we had brought with us this far were left behind in the train, and with them, at last, our illusions.

Every two yards or so an SS man held his tommy gun trained on us. Hand in hand we followed the crowd.

An SS noncommissioned officer came to meet us, a truncheon in his hand. He gave the order:

'Men to the left! Women to the right!'

Eight words spoken quietly, indifferently, without emotion. Eight short, simple words. Yet that was the moment when I parted from my mother. I had not had time to think, but already I felt the pressure of my father's hand: we were alone. For part of a second I glimpsed my mother and my sisters moving away to the right. Tzipora held Mother's hand. I saw them disappear into the distance ; my mother was stroking my sister's fair hair, as though to protect her, while I walked on with my father and the other men. And I did not know that in that place, at that moment, I was parting from my mother and Tzipora forever. I went on walking. My father held on to my hand.

UNDERSTANDING OF READING TASK

Follow these instructions to help you develop and express your response:

1 Select four or five words or phrases from each text which convey, to you, the personal thoughts and feelings of the narrator. Discuss with a partner the literal meaning of these words or phrases and the implied meanings.

2 These texts use a range of sentence constructions. Find and discuss:
   - A short sentence written for greater impact
   - A complex sentence. What effect does this sentence have at that point in the text?
   - A sentence which does not follow the expected 'rules' of a sentence. Why has the author chosen to include this?

What effect does the sentence have on the reader?

3 Based on your findings about the narrator's personal thoughts and feelings, try to describe the **tone** of the writing. What **voice** do you 'hear' reading it? (What kind of person is speaking? How would you describe the tone of voice they use?)

How much do you come to know about the author of each? Compare these with what you find out about the writer in the poem 'In The Attic'.

How effectively does each writer communicate their feelings about the experiences they describe in these extracts?

WRITING TASK

- Write about a member of your own family whom you have not seen for some time. Select either poetry or prose and try to include some of the techniques evident in the texts you have studied here.

- Once you have completed your writing, swop with a partner. Read their piece of writing and identify the techniques used from this section. Discuss your findings.

TEXT DETECTIVES

Read the following extracts all of which are from fiction texts. Can you determine the genre of each from such a short extract?

To help you, consider the following:

- the title of the novel, given in brackets after the extract
- the events which have taken place or are now taking place
- the characters – names, personalities, actions and responses
- the setting of the extract and other settings referred to
- your experience of the conventions of certain genres.

Look carefully for the clues and refer to your conventions chart from the previous page. The Fictional Genre Grid below might be helpful.

FICTIONAL GENRE GRID			
Detective	Science fiction	Romance	Comedy
Crime	Horror	Adventure	Spoof
Thriller	Fantasy	Sport	
Murder Mystery	Ghost		

A

'I'm listening.' Gib came into the room and sat down in my chair. I sat at the edge of my bed.

'Well, I was thinking about how I'd try to get money from the bank,' I said eagerly. 'If I didn't have access to the cashiers' user accounts and I could write a program to do it, I reckon it would be quite simple – if I knew exactly what I was doing.'

'Go on.'

'I'd change a noddy program days before it was needed, to contain one of those time-trap things Dad was talking about. One of the programs that runs every night. Then, on a certain day at a certain time, the money would get transferred.'

'I get you,' Gib said, leaning forward. 'But how would you get round the acceptance testers? They check all the source programs to make sure there's nothing in them that shouldn't be there.'

(*Hacker*)

B

One of the things Ford Prefect had always found hardest to understand about humans was their habit of continually stating and repeating the very, very obvious, as in *It's a nice day*, or *You're very tall*, or *Oh dear you seem to have fallen down a thirty-foot well, are you alright?* At first Ford had formed a theory to account for this strange behaviour. If human beings don't keep exercising their lips, he thought, their mouths probably seize up. After a few months' consideration and observation he abandoned this theory in favour of a new one. If they don't keep exercising their lips, he thought, their brains start working. After a while he abandoned this one as well as being obstructively cynical and decided he quite liked human beings after all, but he always remained desperately worried about the terrible number of things they didn't know about.

(*The Hitch Hiker's Guide to the Galaxy*)

C

He couldn't save Jessie. He daren't save Jessie. His hoarse sobs and coughs scattered the mice in the old loft. He had never cried so much before. He had never realised what a coward he was. Every time he thought of going to Lambton Police Station and saying what he had done, he imagined the blindfold being tied roughly round his eyes by the hangman at Derby Gaol. He could imagine the rough rope being fastened round his neck, cutting a little as the hangman got it into position. Then the sudden pain and darkness for ever and ever. He could not do it, not even for Jessie. He could not. But then he heard Jessie's screams and heard her in his mind calling out to him, and he could stand it no longer. He crept down the ladder and fetched one of the shining brass stable lanterns. The boys were forbidden to take the lanterns into the lofts because of the risk of the fire in the hay, but John did not care any more. He returned with the lantern to his loft. At least it stopped the worst of his imaginings.

(*The Throttlepenny Murder*)

D

'Where are the gyptians?' she said. 'Is John Faa safe? Did they fight off the Samoyeds?'

'Most of them are safe. John Faa is wounded, though not severely. The men who took you were hunters and raiders who often prey on parties of travellers, and alone they can travel more quickly than a large party. The gyptians are still a day's journey away.'

The two boys were staring in fear at the goose- daemon and at Lyre's familiar manner with him, because of course they'd never seen a daemon without his human before, and they knew little about witches.

(*Northern Lights*)

Complete a genre analysis for each extract. Include specific references to the genre conventions you have identified.
Include details and evidence for each of the discussion points suggested at the beginning of this section.

Read the following opening chapter to a novel written by Robert E. Swindells.

The Ghost Messengers

'Meg came awake again and opened her eyes and he was there again – a silhouette against the curtain. She couldn't see his face but she knew it was him. He had appeared from time to time like this ever since she could remember: watching her with his sad eyes. He never spoke. Once or twice she'd whispered, 'Grandad?' but he hadn't answered her. Perhaps he couldn't. Ghosts in stories shriek and moan, but that's in stories. Perhaps when you're dead you have no voice.

She lay still, gazing at him across the dim room. She was not afraid. When he began to fade she smiled. She liked to think it made him happy to see her smile, but since he never spoke there was no way of knowing.

When he'd gone she lay staring up into the dark. Where did he go, she wondered, when he left her? Did he go wherever it was his bones lay? Was he unhappy because nobody knew where they were? Might he have rested better if they'd found his bomber and buried him properly?

The darkness about her seemed full of moving things and her eyelids grew heavy, and yet she didn't sleep. She couldn't, because a part of her had followed the phantom and was out there somewhere, wandering. Those of us who sleep soundly are more fortunate than we know, for it is a fact that two sorts of spirits haunt the night: those of the restless dead, and the spirits of those who live, and know no rest.

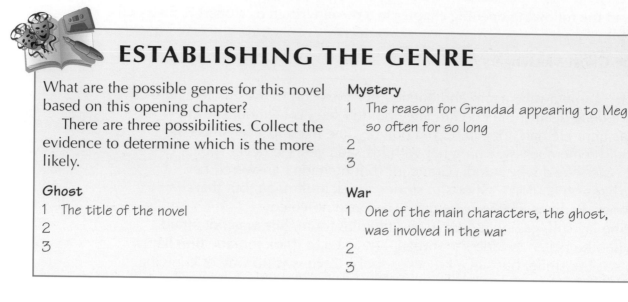

ESTABLISHING THE GENRE

What are the possible genres for this novel based on this opening chapter?

There are three possibilities. Collect the evidence to determine which is the more likely.

Ghost

1   The title of the novel

2

3

Mystery

1   The reason for Grandad appearing to Meg so often for so long

2

3

War

1   One of the main characters, the ghost, was involved in the war

2

3

Based on your **evidence**, what is your decision? Write your opinion, with reasons and evidence, in less than 150 words. Organise a class vote or debate.

UNDERSTANDING OF READING TASK

Answer the following questions in the time allocated:

1   Why is this opening chapter so unusually short? What effect does this have on the reader?

2   Explore the impact or effect of the following use of language:
   • Meg *came* awake
   • *but that's in stories*
   • the *phantom*
   • Those of *us* who sleep soundly
   • *and know no rest*

3   Why, do you think, does Grandad choose to visit Meg? How does she feel about this?

4   Why has the author included so many unanswered questions in this chapter?

5   What is the mood of this chapter?

Remember! Questions like these in the examination mark your knowledge and understanding of the reading material. With at least one other person, list the range of features you could comment on in a text to show your knowledge and understanding.

BECOME AN EXAMINER

Use the following guide to the National Curriculum levels to mark your partner's answers:

Below Level 4
- answers are likely to be brief or narrative
- a few points will show some understanding of content and structure
- misunderstandings will be evident

Level 4
- largely narrative answers but selection of points will be relevant
- some references to the text
- a few comments about structure with a brief explanation

Level 5
- explanations will show a general understanding of links/way it is written/effectiveness
- ability to recognise the build up of detail
- ideas are illustrated by textual references
- may refer to particular words or phrases
- some awareness of effects

Level 6
- begins to explore structure
- answers rooted in the text
- aware of links/effectiveness and the way it is written
- comments are detailed in places
- views supported by the text
- aware of the writer's use of language

Level 7
- explains structure
- answers rooted in the text or supported by well-selected references
- clear understanding of links, writer's style and the use of the language
- full answers show an engagement with the text

About Level 7
- an analytical answer
- appreciation of structure
- coherent reading of the text
- discussion of aspects of language and structure
- skilful use of references

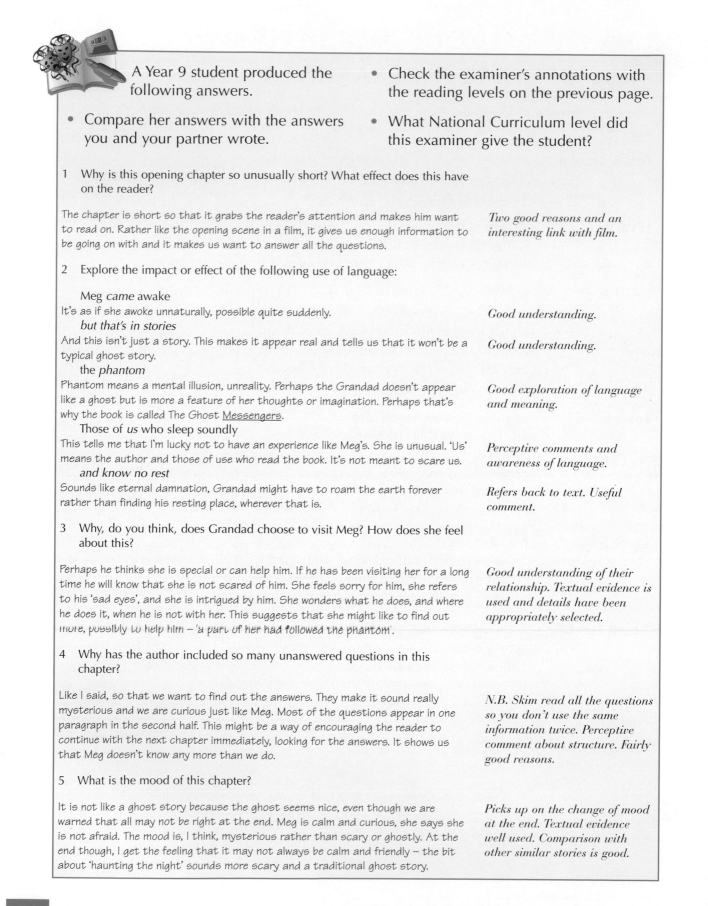

A Year 9 student produced the following answers.

- Compare her answers with the answers you and your partner wrote.

- Check the examiner's annotations with the reading levels on the previous page.

- What National Curriculum level did this examiner give the student?

1   Why is this opening chapter so unusually short? What effect does this have on the reader?

The chapter is short so that it grabs the reader's attention and makes him want to read on. Rather like the opening scene in a film, it gives us enough information to be going on with and it makes us want to answer all the questions.

Two good reasons and an interesting link with film.

2   Explore the impact or effect of the following use of language:

Meg *came* awake
It's as if she awoke unnaturally, possible quite suddenly.

Good understanding.

but that's in stories
And this isn't just a story. This makes it appear real and tells us that it won't be a typical ghost story.

Good understanding.

the *phantom*
Phantom means a mental illusion, unreality. Perhaps the Grandad doesn't appear like a ghost but is more a feature of her thoughts or imagination. Perhaps that's why the book is called The Ghost Messengers.

Good exploration of language and meaning.

Those of *us* who sleep soundly
This tells me that I'm lucky not to have an experience like Meg's. She is unusual. 'Us' means the author and those of use who read the book. It's not meant to scare us.

Perceptive comments and awareness of language.

and know no rest
Sounds like eternal damnation, Grandad might have to roam the earth forever rather than finding his resting place, wherever that is.

Refers back to text. Useful comment.

3   Why, do you think, does Grandad choose to visit Meg? How does she feel about this?

Perhaps he thinks she is special or can help him. If he has been visiting her for a long time he will know that she is not scared of him. She feels sorry for him, she refers to his 'sad eyes', and she is intrigued by him. She wonders what he does, and where he does it, when he is not with her. This suggests that she might like to find out more, possibly to help him – 'a part of her had followed the phantom'.

Good understanding of their relationship. Textual evidence is used and details have been appropriately selected.

4   Why has the author included so many unanswered questions in this chapter?

Like I said, so that we want to find out the answers. They make it sound really mysterious and we are curious just like Meg. Most of the questions appear in one paragraph in the second half. This might be a way of encouraging the reader to continue with the next chapter immediately, looking for the answers. It shows us that Meg doesn't know any more than we do.

N.B. Skim read all the questions so you don't use the same information twice. Perceptive comment about structure. Fairly good reasons.

5   What is the mood of this chapter?

It is not like a ghost story because the ghost seems nice, even though we are warned that all may not be right at the end. Meg is calm and curious, she says she is not afraid. The mood is, I think, mysterious rather than scary or ghostly. At the end though, I get the feeling that it may not always be calm and friendly – the bit about 'haunting the night' sounds more scary and a traditional ghost story.

Picks up on the change of mood at the end. Textual evidence well used. Comparison with other similar stories is good.

IMPROVING YOUR NARRATIVE WRITING SKILLS

NARRATIVES: WRITING TO IMAGINE, EXPLORE OR ENTERTAIN

Narratives are not just stories written in prose.

Have you read a poem which tells a story – such as *The Pied Piper of Hamelin* or *The Lady of Shalott*? Have you ever read a play script – such as *Chicken Run* or *The Roses of Eyam*? These forms of writing are also narratives.

Think about narrative structures. There are many ways of organising a narrative but generally this is the format they follow:

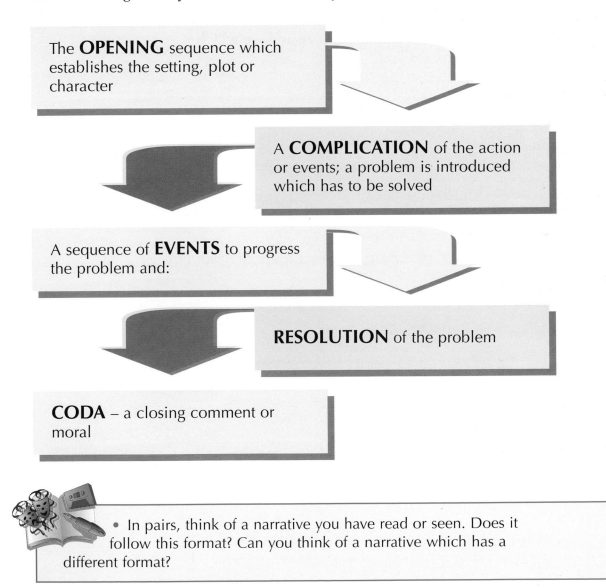

The **OPENING** sequence which establishes the setting, plot or character

A **COMPLICATION** of the action or events; a problem is introduced which has to be solved

A sequence of **EVENTS** to progress the problem and:

RESOLUTION of the problem

CODA – a closing comment or moral

- In pairs, think of a narrative you have read or seen. Does it follow this format? Can you think of a narrative which has a different format?

PLANNING A NARRATIVE (Part 1)

Know what to write before you start! Even in an examination, when you might be afraid of wasting time, it is important to plan your writing in order to write an effective narrative. Remember that examination markers have a lot of narratives to mark. Yours needs to be interesting and not just another story to read and grade.

There are different ways of planning a narrative. You need to know which is the best way for you. We are not all the same, so don't just plan a narrative the way your friend does it!

There will be a selection of narrative possibilities on this section of the examination paper. Some planning methods are better suited to a particular style. Look at the following suggestions for good combinations.

Try one or more of these just as planning exercises. There is no need to write the narrative; just complete the plan and see which is the easiest or most productive for you.

THE MINDMAP

You have probably used this method before. It is a way of writing down a whole range of ideas, which come to your mind in a short space of time.

Narrative examination style: the opening line is given for you to continue.

Anna looked up from her magazine, just in time to see Mark disappear through the doorway…

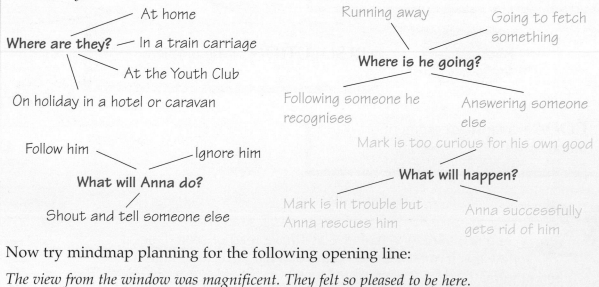

Now try mindmap planning for the following opening line:

The view from the window was magnificent. They felt so pleased to be here.

THE LIST

A useful planning process when you have a lot of details or ideas to include.

Narrative examination style: the eye-witness account or when a subject or topic is given.

Give an account of a person who has been a positive influence for you.

My cousin Sam
Why? – has overcome physical difficulties resulting from an accident three
years ago

- has never grumbled about the accident or blamed anyone else
- made several good friends in hospital and still keeps in touch
- remains positive about himself
- tries to carry on at school even though he can't walk easily
- doesn't stop his friends doing things because he can't any more
- attends physiotherapy regularly even though it is difficult

Now try planning in list form for this topic:

Imagine you saw the evacuation of your area due to an unexploded World War Two bomb. Write an eye-witness account of this experience, making it as convincing and detailed as possible.

THE MAP

This is a way of thinking along certain lines, following a train of thought rather than allowing your mind to skip around. On paper this looks rather like a road map with main roads and junctions leading off.

Narrative examination style: the genre is given to you

Mystery

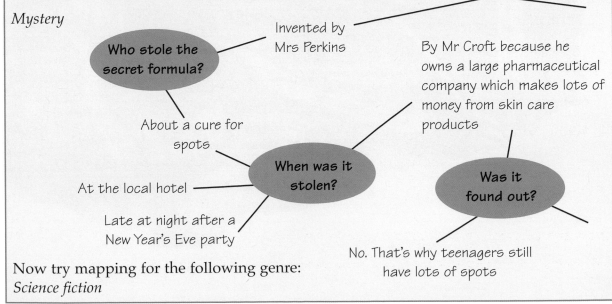

Now try mapping for the following genre:
Science fiction

SELECTING WHICH TO DO

In an examination you have little time to decide what it is you want to write about. You will not have time to plan fully each option presented to you so you must:

1 Quickly think about the possibilities for each one.
2 Decide which ONE to attempt based on your immediate preference and which option you think will enable you to write well.
3 Plan that option using one of the techniques on this page and the previous one.

PLANNING A NARRATIVE (Part 2)

You are now in the lucky position of having lots of ideas – but you can't include them all! In an exam you have a limit to your time available and it is important that you don't overrun your time in one section because that will affect the quality of your answers or writing in the next section.

The narrative you write needs to be complete within the time allowed. Don't select a complex plot with a huge number of characters. Keep it simple.

You will now need to select from the ideas you have recorded. Which ideas do you want to include? Remember, you can't use them all.

Look at the **mindmap** about Anna and Mark or your own mindmap. Put a circle around one idea in each category starting with the aspect which is most significant for you. For example:

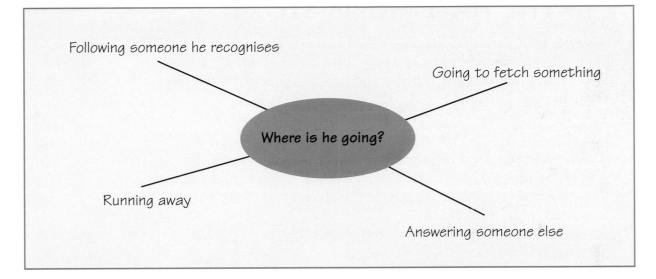

Now look at the other aspects of this narrative. Which ideas will tie in with this starting point? You might have to decide quickly on some different details rather than keep rigidly to those you have jotted down. In this way you can group together all the details needed for this narrative. Cross out those ideas you reject.

If you have **mapped** your ideas you will probably have all the elements of your narrative already in front of you if you thought logically as you recorded the ideas. If not, you will need to tick the ideas you wish to use and cross out the rejected ideas much as you would for a brainstorm plan.

In a **list** you have in front of you a number of points you are going to include. Cross out those you don't want to include. Now think about which points link on together quite well. You could link these together with arrows.

Your next decision is about the **sequence** of events. Where do you start? What makes a good opening?

Is it necessary to start at the beginning of events – or could you start with the ending and then tell your reader how it all came to happen? Would you prefer to introduce the main character first – or the setting?

What details will you include in your first paragraph – a description of the setting, something happening, the main character talking?

Look again at your plan and number the ideas in the sequence in which they appear in your narrative. Think about the ending really carefully. Aim for a strong or thought-provoking ending. Don't let it just stop. Keep your reader's attention right to the very end.

THE HALF-HOUR STORY

Now write your narrative, for one of the plans you have created, in 30 minutes. (In an examination you would have slightly longer. 35 minutes are recommended, but you are expected to spend 5 minutes on thinking and planning.)

Remember to:

- Follow your plan and cross the item off as you finish writing it.
- Check the time you have available if this is in timed conditions.
- Have an interesting opening paragraph which clearly establishes character, plot or setting.
- Make the final paragraph strong and memorable, perhaps even teasing your reader.

After this period of time you will be able to check your writing for errors in spelling and punctuation.

HOW GOOD IS MY NARRATIVE?

You may find that you don't always know whether your own writing is going to get a high mark or not.

BECOME AN EXAMINER

Read this opening paragraph written by a Year 9 student in examination conditions. Read it by yourself and then discuss it with a partner.

The wind was chill tonight, as it howled and knifed down the country lanes and set all the leaves whipping like dervishes in a frenzy. Trees swayed gracefully in the vicious gusts and the branches that arched over the roads gave occasional threatening creaks. I slammed on the brakes of my old Bentley for the fifteenth time and heard Madeline's irritable sigh from the back seat.

'Must you keep stopping every time we come to a tree, Nigel?'

'Don't exaggerate,' I snapped back. 'Do you or do you not want to get to the party in one piece?' She gave a deep, dramatic groan.

'So this is what comes of being married to a detective? Every tree has its motive – now it only needs the opportunity ... Oh, just get on, Nigel. We'll be late!'

Is this opening effective? Does it:

- establish the genre?
- introduce the main characters?
- provide some description?
- establish the setting or the events to follow?
- use language in an effective way?

Now read the whole narrative written by your partner.
What National Curriculum level would you give it? Use the
phrases in the grid below to identify the level it achieves, in your opinion.

Below Level 4	- some ideas clearly expressed - has shape and an ending - basic grammar is correct - some punctuation is used accurately - spelling of simple words is usually accurate
Level 4	- ideas are clear - mostly organised into a narrative or appropriate form - some use of complex sentences - beginning to use vocabulary effectively - punctuation mostly accurate
Level 5	- clearly expressed and structured appropriately - tries to engage the reader through descriptions, etc. - reasonably wide vocabulary - simple and complex sentences used - range of punctuation used - spelling is usually accurate for simple and complex regular patterns
Level 6	- writing is interesting and engaging in parts - uses an appropriate style - varied vocabulary - range of sentence constructions and appropriate paragraphing used effectively - punctuation is used to clarify meaning - there may be spelling errors for difficult words
Level 7	- writing is confident, organised - appropriate and engaging style and tone - interest is built up - sequence of ideas - range of grammatical features - effective use of vocabulary - spelling correct
About Level 7	- seeks to engage and maintain interest - ideas and events coherent - precise use of vocabulary - style and structure enables clarity - consistent grasp of paragraphing and punctuation - spelling is correct

What have you noticed about these marking levels? What do you need to do in order to
gain a high level?

IMPROVING YOUR WRITING

Look again at the opening paragraph or two of the narrative you have written. How could it be improved? Work with a partner to make changes to your narrative opening. Remember, this is your opportunity to impress your reader!

Set yourself a target for improvement.

Make sure it is clear, achievable and something you feel able to work on.

Now read the rest of the narrative written by a Year 9 student. Refresh your memory by re-reading the opening, on the previous page, first.

I turned carefully away and grimaced at the windscreen. Slowly I edged forwards, feeling the life crackle through the veins of my old beauty. She was all I really worried about as I slipped beneath the creaking boughs. Whether Madeline was late for her wretched pagan festival made no difference to me. Especially since she took such pleasure in ridiculing everything I did, attributing it to the natural distrust I had of everything vaguely abnormal. Now, as she leaned over the back seat, to put the finishing touches to her grotesque witch make-up, she glanced sideways.

'Do you intend to stay in first gear all the way to Valerie's?' she enquired.

'No dear,' I muttered, 'I just thought you might like a little extra time to put your make-up on, that's all.'

She glared at me and pulled back, warts and pustules and all, to the back seat. With an hardly audible sigh, I changed gear.

It had been Madeline's idea to accept the invitation to Valerie's Halloween 'do.' I would much rather have stayed at home and sorted through the paperwork of my last case, but she had insisted, with much pouting and complaining, that I hardly every did anything for her. I deemed it unwise to mention the new Fiesta sitting in the driveway of our Bristol home, or the show we'd recently been to see for her birthday, because I knew she would have a perfectly good retort waiting. So here I was, driving along a narrow Somerset lane in my beloved Bentley, dressed in tacky, corner-shop Count Dracula get-up, with tomato sauce around my mouth and Madeline's bright red lipstick on. I felt a total fool and had, contrary to my usual habits, been staying religiously inside the speed limit. No policemen would go back to the station, laughing, because of me!

Eventually, Lindly Hoe came into sight. It was an Elizabethan manor house, set at the end of a snaking drive that writhed through a skeletal avenue of oak trees. With the full October moon hovering over the ramparts, it looked the very place for a Halloween party. Cars thronged the gravelled area outside the door and all kinds of Gothic monsters trailed up the front steps to the entrance. I steeled myself for an evening of useless small-talk, meaningless smiles and polite compliments, and brought the Bentley into third gear.

In order to assess the quality of this narrative we need to consider the kinds of features we have looked at so far in this unit. We have looked at:

1 Identifying vocabulary which has been used to create a very specific idea or response and the effect created.

2 Identifying the range or punctuation used and its effect, if appropriate.

3 Identifying at least one simple and one complex sentence and describing the effects they have.

4 Creating:
   • Setting. Identify the words and phrases which describe the route of the journey and where they are going.
   • Characters. There are only two main characters and another named but unknown character. How much do we know about these two and their relationship? How are we given this information?
   • Plot. The narrative is very simple and ends with their arrival but no details of the party itself. Think about the effectiveness of the ending.

5 The structure of this narrative is interesting because details gradually build up as you read on. For example, we are told early on that the man is a detective. Half-way through, we hear he would prefer to be sorting his paperwork for his last case. Shortly after, we learn that he is driving carefully so that he's not stopped by the police and seen in his fancy dress gear.

Trace the emergence of the following details and discuss the effect this technique has on the plot and the reader.
   • the way the characters are dressed
   • the party they are going to
   • the time of year.

6 Check the accuracy and difficulty of the spelling.

➡ In pairs, allocate a National Curriculum level to this narrative and give your reasoning in writing, giving precise details and supporting evidence.

Remember!

The English Test Paper 1 section B is a test of fictional
READING.

- Read your instructions carefully and keep to the task you
  have been set.
- Consider all the aspects listed for you as guidance.
- Your answers in Section A must be clearly based on the
  text and evidence included as quotations.
- Aim to show your understanding of the text.
- Refer directly to the language used, and the effect it has,
  whenever possible.

The English Test Paper 1 Section C is a test of narrative and
other forms of **WRITING**.

- Select your chosen task quickly.
- Plan your writing before you start.
- Keep to a plan which is achievable in the time allocated.
- Aim to complete your task and allow time to check your
  writing.
- PLAN, WRITE, CHECK.

Always keep an eye on the clock and use the time allowed as
suggested on the front of the examination paper.

WHAT NEXT?

In this unit you have studied and revised ways in which writers write different types of narrative texts. To help you with your revision for the reading and writing tests, work individually or with a partner to answer the following questions:

- What are the benefits of first person narrative?
- What are the benefits of third person narrative?
- Write a short definition of the word 'genre'.
- Most narratives have a similar structure. Try to describe the most common forms of narrative structure.
- Write down three different ways of starting a narrative.
- List the range of word and sentence features you could comment on when writing about narrative.

TEN TOP TIPS

Write yourself a list of Top Ten Tips for narrative writing. Use these as a revision checklist. The first is done for you; the next three have been started for you. Now complete the list:

1. If it is going to be interesting to read, it should be interesting to write. If I get bored with writing I need to re-consider my plot and writing style.
2. The plot…
3. The characters…
4. The opening…
5.
6.
7.
8.
9.
10.

UNIT FIVE

Investigating Non-Narrative Texts

The aim of this unit is to:
- focus on non-narrative text types
- prepare for the National Curriculum tests in English
- enable you to target specific areas of your work to improve.

As you work through this unit you will develop your skills as:

SPEAKERS AND LISTENERS

by working with a partner collaboratively and as a critical friend
by considering the effectiveness of language in a range of texts

READERS

by reading a variety of written forms and considering the conventions of each
by exploring meaning and understanding of texts

WRITERS

by developing your skills to writing a non-narrative text in examination conditions
by peer and self marking of written comprehension
by identifying specific aspects to include in analysis and 'writing in the style of' exercises
by reading the work of other students and judging the content using the writing frame
by considering target audience as an essential feature in written material

Turn the page to open up a world of writing, which you probably take for granted. How many forms of writing do you think you come across everyday?

DIFFERENT WRITING FORMATS

The amount of different writing styles and formats we come into contact with during a typical week, both in and out of school, is sometimes surprising. These range, for example, from the nutritional grid on the side of a cereal packet to instructions for downloading a game cheat from the Internet.

Not convinced? Keep a diary of all the writing forms you read during a period of three or four days. Compare your results with a partner. Include everything you read, wherever you read it.

- In a group, list the variety of writing forms you know or have used in English, either this year or during the past two or more years.

Start with these: **autobiography, summary, letter, report**

- Now add the different writing formats you have used in other subjects.

- Select one of the items from your list for discussion with a partner. What is involved in this form of writing? What would it look like on the page? When is it used?

INVESTIGATING NON-NARRATIVE FORMS

You can improve your writing of different types of non-narrative writing if you can investigate the key features of each form.
Over the next few pages, you will explore the following types of writing and develop your skills in writing each one:

- newspaper article
- information leaflet
- travel writing
- discussion essay.

Before you begin to focus on each one, spend a few minutes listing what you already know about the characteristics of and differences between these types of writing.

THE DAILY NEWS: writing to inform, persuade or comment

WRITING A NEWSPAPER ARTICLE

Newspapers are read by millions of people each day and therefore have to appeal to an extremely broad readership. Their target audience is clearly identifiable. The purpose of the writing varies greatly though. Some articles are written in order to inform the reader, others wish to influence, or persuade, the reader. Some features in a newspaper, especially at weekends, give reviews and comments.

A newspaper is cheap and disposable. It has to work hard at grabbing the reader's attention – and holding it. Its impact must be immediate or it will not be bought. Every word and every picture is selected with the utmost care.

By reading the writing in the table and looking at the article on the next page you will find out more about the way newspaper articles are written.

Form	Newspaper articles	
Purpose	To present current affairs and other information in an accessible form	
Types and examples	Tabloid	emphasis on sensational stories, magazine-type articles
	Broadsheet	emphasis on political and economic stories
	Local	emphasis on events and concerns of the local area
	National	emphasis on large-scale items with a pre-dominance of London based items
Text organisation	**Headline**: gives the outline of the story. The choice of words will indicate the nature of the story, e.g. sad, amusing.	
	First half of the article: the first paragraph will be an expansion of the headline. The second paragraph will add more details. After that, each paragraph in the first half will give further information.	
	Second half of the article: will give details not necessarily part of the main story. Often includes interviews and 'human interest' elements or a refresher of yesterday's story.	
	Final paragraph: will either anticipate the next stage of the story or link this story to other similar stories or issues.	
	Caption to photographs or illustration: will explain the content of the picture.	
Language features	Written in the third person	
	Range of tenses used	
	Use of connectives	
	Vocabulary will be suited to the assumed readership – tabloids, simpler than the broadsheets	
	Sentences can be long and complex with use of commas to separate elements	
	Paragraphs –two or three sentences long	
	Use of emotive or eye-catching words in headlines	
	Captions use straight-forward language	
	Reporter often gives personal opinion	
	Use of direct quotation and reported speech	

Now read the article on the following page.

Warning: Delays likely, iguana ahead

For the drivers fuming in a three-mile tailback on the A67, it seemed like just another hold-up on Britain's chock-a-block roads.

But this was no ordinary traffic jam caused by anything as mundane as road repairs or a broken-down lorry.

This particular traffic stopper, making herself at home on the approach to Teeside Airport, was a three-foot iguana called Izzie – hardly a native of the North-East.

Snaking along the white lines, the roaming reptile was on the road to freedom after escaping when her owner, building worker Peter Millward, took her to work and left a window open.

Police patrolman Kevin Marshall arrived at the scene and, armed with a dust sheet, managed to capture the runaway.

The lizard was then bundled into a police car and returned to Mr Millward, 32, of Newton Aycliffe, Co Durham, who had reported the pet missing a month earlier.

'I often take Izzie to work with me and I had been working near the airport when she went missing,' he explained.

'I had left her in a room with the window down to get some fresh air and she squeezed out. Thankfully, there was plenty of vegetation in the area for her to eat – otherwise she might never have survived.'

PC Stuart Moore faced an altogether weightier problem when he went to investigate another three-mile tailback – this time on the A3 near Petersfield, Hampshire.

A one-ton bull called Eric had decided to take a walk into town along the dual carriageway. Not surprisingly, there weren't too many drivers keen to risk over-taking.

PC Moore managed to force the Charolais bull down a side road, where he was cornered and rounded up at Bariton Business Park.

Farmer Nicholas Atkinson, 38, described Eric, who is thought to have escaped from his field through a hole in the hedge, as 'a normally placid chap'.

He added: 'The heat may have been a bit too much for him. He's looking after ten heifers at the moment.'

From the Daily Mail Tuesday, July 27, 1999

READING TASK

In pairs, discuss the following. Make notes as you work through these questions.

THE HEADLINE

1 What does the phrase 'delays likely' usually refer to? Why was it chosen for this article?

2 What is the tone of the headline? What sort of story is this likely to be?

THE PICTURE

1 Why has this picture been included for this story?

2 Why doesn't it have a caption, even though it was originally part of the article?

THE ARTICLE

1 Compare the headline and the opening paragraph. What new information are you given?

2 Read the first five paragraphs of the article (up to '… who had reported his pet missing a month earlier.')

3 List all of the **facts** in this section of the article.

4 How much of this first half of the article is the reporter's **opinion**? Write down the opinions you can find.

5 Read the second half of the article. How much more does this tell you about the actual news item, the capture of the runaway iguana?

6 How many different stories are there in this news article? How are they linked together?

7 How many different people were interviewed for this article? Why were these people selected?

8 How many sentences are there in each paragraph?

9 Make a list of any words you are unfamiliar with. What does this indicate about the reading difficulty of this article.

10 This is a 'fun', light-hearted news story. Can you find any examples of language being used in a particular way? For instance, 'Snaking along the white lines' – a description of the iguana which uses an image of another reptile for effect. Discuss your finding with another pair in your class.

WRITING TASK

- Write your own newspaper article using the techniques that have emerged from your study of the 'iguana ahead' article.

- Remember:
  - who will read it (your target audience)
  - the headline
  - ideas for photographs and their captions
  - where the factual information will appear
  - who might be quoted
  - how it will end.

The following is a newspaper article – but its content is rather different to the iguana article. The iguana story had a rather amusing but actual incident which it wished to inform its readers of. How much fact appears in the following newspaper article?

Read the article carefully in order to consider the information it contains.

Ali's treetop tiger tussle

When Subedar Aii, 29, an elephant handler at the Corbett National Park, India, was attacked by a tiger in February 1984, he felt his last moments had come. Ali, foraging for animal fodder with his colleague Qutub and two elephants, was up a tree a short distance away from his workmate when the tiger pounced and pulled him to the ground.

The animal grabbed the back of Ali's neck, then bit off the top of his scalp. As it chewed at the morsel, Ali tried to scramble away, but a swat from the tiger's huge paw pinned his leg quite firmly to the ground.

Ali knew that nothing he could do would make matters worse. Inches away from the huge animal, and enveloped in an all pervasive catty stench, he grabbed its tongue. The cat looked perplexed and then promptly bit his hand. Howling in agony, the elephant handler began to beat at the tiger's head with his other hand.

Dragged into forest

Rather than killing him instantly the tiger merely swept a magisterial paw across Ali's face, and then sank its teeth into his back, dragging him into the forest. It dropped him and paused. It seemed puzzled by its rebellious prey.

Ali seized this moment to call for help, but his companion Qutub dismissed his desperate cry as a practical joke. Fortunately, at that moment, his elephant caught the tiger's scent and reeled in terror. Qutub, atop his mount, lumbered toward Ali, shouting angrily at the savage predator. Alarmed, it backed away, allowing Ali time to call for his own elephant, who bent down low to let him crawl to safety on its back.

Ali's encounter with the tiger cost him six months in a local hospital, but its encounter with Ali cost the tiger its freedom. After the attack it was captured and spent the rest of its life in an Indian zoo.

UNDERSTANDING OF READING TASK: FACT OR FICTION?

1 What was the original story in this piece of writing?
Re-read the article and decide what actually happened. Jot down in note form the basic details from the article.

2 Using only these facts, re-write this story using 100 words only, including your title. You will need to write it in the style of a newspaper article. Remind yourself of the conventions of newspaper writing on page 103.

A LEAFLET:
Writing to inform, persuade or comment

Households across the country receive leaflets through their door or included within their newspaper or magazine every week. How many of these leaflets do you actually read through?

The following extract from a leaflet asks you to donate money for developing water supplies in another country. It is published by Water Aid. You have probably seen leaflets like this before.

Will you change life for good?

For a child?

Every day, 25,000 children in the Third World die from dirty water. In the time it took you to read this paragraph, another three vulnerable youngsters died.

For whole communities?

Whole communities will benefit from your regular gift. No longer will childhood ailments like diarrhoea be killers. No longer will mothers need to live in fear.

Yet a gift of just £2 a month from you can help bring a whole family a supply of safe, clean water that can last a lifetime. Your gift could be the difference between life and death.

Can you honestly think of a way your £2 a month could do <u>more</u> good, <u>for</u> good?

WaterAid Leaflet

WRITING TASK

The extract you see above is only part of one side of the A4 leaflet.
What else do you think was on this leaflet? What do appeals leaflets usually include?
Complete the leaflet to fill a whole page. What would go in the unfilled space?
Draw the layout and indicate content in boxes. Afterwards, compare leaflets – how similar are they? Why is that? Make a list of the key features of **leaflets**.

EXTENDING YOUR UNDERSTANDING

Collect leaflets from home and bring in to school.

- Divide the leaflets you collect into different categories. These categories might include **information leaflets, appeals leaflets, public service leaflets** and **special offer/sales leaflets.**

- Investigate the differences between different types of leaflet.

DESCRIPTIVE WRITING: Writing to inform, persuade or comment

Think of a place you know well … school! Yes, why not? If you had to inform people about your school you would end up with something like your school prospectus. Have you ever read your school prospectus? If not, ask for a copy and read it, you never know what you might find out!

UNDERSTANDING OF READING TASK

Try to answer the following questions based on the school prospectus only, not your knowledge of the school.

1 Who is the prospectus aimed at, who is the **target audience**? Why do you think this is?
2 What picture of life and study at your school does it give? How does it achieve this?
3 What details are not included? Why is this?
4 Would the prospectus encourage you to come to this school? If not, what else would it need to include?

WRITING TASK

- Select a passage from your school prospectus – a long paragraph will do. Re-write this for a different target audience. How about: the students? visiting foreign educationalists? a prospective buyer? What will you have to change: the content? the tone? the descriptive language used?

- Mark your partner's piece of writing, using the National Curriculum criteria on page 96. How well did you do?

TRAVEL WRITING: Writing to inform, describe, persuade or comment

Modern technology has made it easy to see and find out about the world we live in. People who travel around the world often feel compelled to write about their experiences. The following extract from *The Lost Continent* records Bill Bryson's thoughts and feelings on his return to his homeland after living in Great Britain for several years.

The Lost Continent by Bill Bryson

I come from Des Moines. Somebody had to.

When you come from Des Moines you either accept the fact without question and settle down with a local girl named Bobbi and get a job at the Firestone factory and live there for ever and ever, or you spend your adolescence moaning at length about what a dump it is and how you can't wait to get out, and then you settle down with a local girl named Bobbi and get a job at the Firestone factory and live there for ever and ever.

Hardly anyone ever leaves. This is because Des Moines is the most powerful hypnotic known to man. Outside town there is a big sign that says WELCOME TO DES MOINES. THIS IS WHAT DEATH IS LIKE. There isn't really. I just made that up. But the place does get a grip on you. People who have nothing to do with Des Moines drive in off the interstate, looking for gas or hamburgers, and stay for ever. There's a New Jersey couple up the street from my parents' house whom you see wandering around from time to time looking faintly puzzled but strangely serene. Everybody in Des Moines is strangely serene.

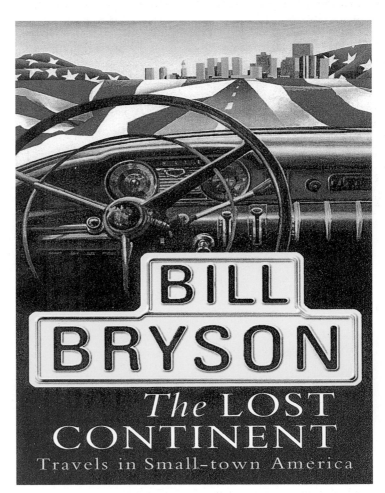

The following extract is from the *AA Book of British Villages*.

HEMINGBROUGH, NORTH YORKSHIRE

Yorkshire's industrial towns robbed Hemingbrough of its importance, and much of its population, during the early part of the 19th century. But the best of its past remains in the main street that runs southwards to the church.

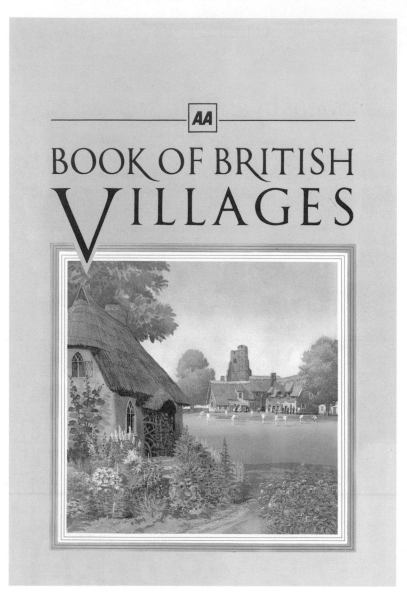

Many of the houses date from the 18th century, and are built of dark-red bricks. A few have been painted in pastel colours. The architecture is simple though often elegant, particularly in the houses close to the church whose 189 ft steeple dominates the village. St Mary's Church was built in the 13th and 15th centuries of white stone quarried at Tadcaster. Its pencil-slim spire soars from a squat tower and is a landmark in the surrounding landscape of flat, open farmland.

The church is known for its bench-end carvings, showing figures of dragons, a monkey and a jester. A misericord – a hinged projection on the underside of a choir seat – dates from about 1200 and is probably the oldest in England.

UNDERSTANDING OF READING TASK

Compare the extracts from *The Lost Continent* and the *AA Book of British Villages*.

- Who is likely to read these texts? How do you know?

- What do they have in common?
- How are they different?

Make detailed notes on their similarities and differences, set out as a grid – for example:

	The Lost Continent	*AA Book Of British Villages*
Viewpoint	Written in the first person	Written in third person
Tone	Informal language	More formal tone
Content		
Purpose		
Audience		
Structure and organisation of the text		

WRITING TASK

Use the area in which you live as the basis for writing in the style of one of these two texts.

- Think carefully about the humour in one and the seriousness of the other.

- Which will be easier for you to copy?

- Who is your target audience?

BOTH SIDES OF THE ARGUMENT: Writing to inform, persuade or comment

You may well have written **persuasively**, when your aim is to convince or persuade your reader of your point of view. However, in this type of writing, you are not just presenting one side of the argument. Your aim is to look at an issue from **different** viewpoints before coming to a conclusion, or making up your mind.

In this type of writing you:

- introduce the subject
- present Point of View 1
- present Point of View 2
- give a conclusion or your personal point of view.

For example:

Introduce the subject

Should animals be kept in zoos?

Every region in this country has at least one zoo which will be visited by thousands of people every year. In these zoos many animals are kept, including many which are born in the zoo as part of their breeding programme. Animal rights organisations say that this is cruel and shouldn't be allowed. The public may agree but this doesn't prevent significant numbers of people paying for a day at the zoo. Is it right that animals are kept in zoos?

Present Point of View 1

Why are zoos considered to be cruel?

Animal rights campaigners argue that it is cruel to keep a wild animal in a small, confined space. Often this is in a country which is not even the natural habitat of the animal …

Present Point of View 2

What is the positive aspect of zoos?

On the other hand, zoos can be the only contact many people have – or can ever have – with animals such as these. Therefore they are highly educational places where …

Conclusion

This is what I think

In conclusion I feel that …

TOP TEN TIPS FOR WRITING A POINT OF VIEW ESSAY

1 Decide on your point of view before writing.

2 Plan your points for and against using the mindmap or list method. (See page 91)

3 Aim for about five different points for each side of the argument.

4 Write an introductory paragraph explaining the issue but do not include any of your points.

5 Write up Point of View 1, your own preference.

6 Write up Point of View 2, giving as much detail as is necessary.

7 Refer to the points made in Point of View 1 when giving Point of View 2.

8 Use language which is more forceful when presenting the point of view you agree with.

9 Show that 'the other side' has a weaker argument by writing a strong counter-argument.

10 Conclude by giving a strong indication of your own point of view. You may not have a clear preference but it is easier to write as if you have!

Select ONE of the following titles for writing in timed conditions:

1 How to make lots of money is the most important thing to consider when deciding on a future career. Do you agree with this viewpoint?

2 Food 'experts' are always giving us scare stories. Do you think that what we eat should be up to us?

3 Do you believe that recycling household materials should be compulsory?

HELP

Planning a point of view essay is important. If you are unsure about possible methods of planning look at the section on planning in Unit Four, pages 90 – 93.

The following incomplete mindmap might be helpful if you are stuck for ideas. Add your own thoughts to develop the plan.

Dwindling world resources

Encouragement is necessary as people hate being told to do things

Recycling – compulsory

Need for different bins

Reduce amount of packaging

The following essay was written by a Year 9 student in 35 minutes as part of an examination preparation. The initial mindmap has not been included.

How to make lots of money is the most important thing to consider when deciding on a future career. Do you agree with this viewpoint?

When speaking to students at any school or college and they are asked their main objectives in life, it is likely that, at some time during their answer, the phrase 'to make a lot of money' will crop up. This ambition is one that is shared by many young people, but will it really bring the happiness they hope for? Does success breed contentment?

Money is, of course, a very important part of life. It can get almost anything done and most people dream of becoming rich. Students long to be able to buy whatever they want whenever they want — new cars, expensive homes, foreign villas etc. Being wealthy can ensure you a comfortable future and a luxurious lifestyle. Years of hard work can be rewarded by getting a 'good' job and bringing money into a family. From this point of view, lots of money is obviously a plus. It can make life easier and infinitely more comfortable.

Yet, on the other hand, we have the old saying 'Money can't buy everything'. It makes sure that life is comfortable but not necessarily happy. As another old saying goes, the more you have the more you want. Once you have started to ascend the scale of wealth, it is hard to stop. To get more money, you would have to work harder — this could lead to the collapse of family life, or even a marriage. Wealth can breed envy and make people fall out of favour with their neighbours or relatives. Frankly, lots of money can cause jealousy and not necessarily ensure the happiness people expect.

Personally, I hope to make a lot of money. I want to live the sort of life that goes shopping to Oxford Street and has at least one foreign holiday home. People may be jealous, but I don't intend to be miserly with my money. I have decided to try and become a lawyer, for the simple reason it is a well-paid job and I have already started looking in estate agents! But I agree with the fact that money can't buy happiness.

In conclusion, people should, I believe, aim as high as they can. The importance of money will never diminish and wealth is something we all dream of.

Read again the essay entitled 'How to make lots of money is the most important thing to consider when deciding on a future career. Do you agree with this viewpoint?'

1 Write down the points which probably appeared on the mindmap for this essay. Use a grid like the one below.

	For	Against
1		
2		
3		
4		
5		

2 How has language been used in this essay?

- Can you find any instances where the words have been deliberately selected in order to be persuasive?

- Which words or phrases have the greatest impact on you as a reader? What is the effect of these words on you?

- Do you get a clear sense of personal belief in the preference stated by the writer?

- Have you been persuaded that the pupil's point of view is the right one to have?

3 Focus on the opening and concluding paragraphs

- How effective is the opening? Does it effectively introduce the subject?

- The writer refers to 'they' rather than 'we'. What effect does this have?

- Why is the writer included in the final paragraph – and what is the effect of that at the end of the essay?

4 Become an examiner

- Use the questions in 2 and 3 above to analyse your own point of view essay.

- Do the same for a partner and give feedback on your thoughts about his or her essay.

- Working with your partner, use the guide to National Curriculum levels on page 96 to decide the level your writing might have been awarded.

- How could your essays have been improved?

WRITING POINT OF VIEW ESSAYS

Set yourself a target for improvement. Make sure it is clear and achievable and something you feel able to work on.

Record this in your exercise book for reference.

SO, WHAT DO YOU KNOW? – BE A TEXT DETECTIVE!

All of the following extracts from texts have been taken from the range of writing forms included in this unit.

Can you identify the writing form in each case? Some are examples of writing forms you have investigated in this unit, others are not! What clues should you look for?

For each extract, identify:
- the target audience
- the overall purpose
- how the text is structured
- key language features
- where the text might have been published.

A
'Muddy Moll'
From the bay-window containing a drinking fountain you can look out over the King's Bath. People of distinction had been coming here long before the city's second flourishing. One of them was James I's consort, Anne of Denmark, or 'Muddy Moll' as the citizens called her, who came to be cured of her dropsy. Instead, she got a nasty shock when the water seemed to explode in flame just as she was getting in. This upset her so much that she went elsewhere to what became known as the Queen's Bath (demolished late last century).

B
24 September, Yorkshire
I blackberry up the lane that leads to Wharfe. A big heron in the beck takes wing and flies slowly away up to Crummock. My nightmare when blackberrying (or when I stop the car for a pee) is that I shall find the body of a child, that I will report it and be suspected of the crime. So I find myself running through in my mind the evidences of my legitimate occupation – where I started picking, who saw me park, and so on.

C
I drive north and west across Michigan, lost in a warm afterglow of pleasure from the museum. I was past Lansing and Grand Rapids and entering the Manistee National Forest, 100 miles away, almost before I knew it. Michigan is shape like an oven mitt and is often about as exciting. The Manistee forest was dense and dull – endless groves of uniform pine trees – and the highway through it was straight and flat. Occasionally I would see a cabin or little lake in the woods, both just glimpsable through the trees, but mostly there was nothing of note. Towns were rare and mostly squalid – scattered dwellings and ugly prefab buildings where they made and sold ugly prefab cabins, so that people could buy their own little bit of ugliness and take it out into the woods.

D

Relish exploring this lovely fortress, one of the South West's most important garrisons. It is an ideal picnic spot and why not visit by taking the Castle Ferry from Dartmouth, along the beautiful wooded banks of the River Dart?

For 600 years Dartmouth Castle has stood in a superb waterfront setting as the guardian of the Dart estuary. One of the most advanced fortresses of its day, the Castle was brilliantly positioned to protect the homes and warehouses of Dartmouth's wealthy medieval merchants.

And in more recent times, the Castle served new defensive roles: you can discover the Victorian gun battery and magazines. Or see the legacy of World War II, when again the fortress protected Dartmouth.

E

Animal lovers were distraught yesterday after losing their battle to save a stranded killer whale.

The 18ft creature was put to sleep after experts decided she was too ill to survive a second attempt to pull her to safety in deep water.

She was given a lethal injection by vet Jeremy Statisfield on the beach at Sandwich, Kent, where she had been washed back ashore after the first rescue attempt.

F

My holiday in Spain started brilliantly. The sun shone all the time and the beach was gorgeous. I spent hours swimming in the sea every day until, one really hot afternoon, things went drastically wrong.

I was out swimming when, suddenly, I felt a heavy weight wrap itself around my ankle. Immediately, pain shot up my leg, as if I was being stung by hundreds of stinging nettles. I couldn't believe how much it hurt and, for a moment, I felt paralysed. I stood up and shook my leg like mad to free it, but whatever it was wouldn't budge and actually seemed to cling on even tighter.

G
This outfit was formed in California largely from ex-backing musicians to the likes of Ricky Nelson, Bob Seger and Linda Ronstadt. They and singing composer Jackson Browne became hip Asylum Records' flagship acts after 1972's *Eagle* spawned three US hit 45s – the first, 'Take It Easy', co-written by Browne – all in popular country-rock vein. More of the same on 1973's thematic *Desperado* and *On The Border* led swiftly to years of national chart-toppers in both the album and singles lists, and more qualified strikes overseas where 1977's 'Hotel California' was the only 45 to reach Britain's Top 10.

H
You haven't done anything wrong, apart from getting in the way of your mum's anger at the wrong time. She's very upset and probably very frightened about the future. She rows with your dad but the anger still builds inside her and she lashes out at anyone else who comes within spitting distance. This means that you're taking the brunt of it, and that obviously isn't fair.

I'm glad that you're seeing a counsellor and it's very important that you tell her about this. It's easy to take what your mum says at face value, but she doesn't means what she says. She's so distressed herself that she can't think at the moment. That's why it's vital you have someone, an adult, that you can talk to.

I
Growing and Demolishing Founded Cities
An existing city can grow to the next size up. Click the *Build* button then, without choosing a city size, click on a street or building in the appropriate city. The city expands to the next largest category, if it has the land to do so. When a city reaches metropolis size, it continues to grow with each click until all the available land is occupied.

Remember!
When you are asked to read or write in any of these non-narrative forms you need to think about:

- genre
- purpose
- target audience
- the way the text is organised
- language features which will be evident.

WHAT NEXT?

In this unit you have studied and revised ways that writers write different types of non-narrative texts. To help you with your revision for the reading and writing tests, work individually or with a partner to answer the following questions:

- What is meant by the term 'target audience'?
- Describe the differences between a 'tabloid' and a 'broadsheet' newspaper.
- What are the key language features of a newspaper report?

- Can you summarise the key features of 'persuasive' writing? Use the following headings to help you:

  - text structure and organisation
  - language features
  - design/layout features
  - target audience.

As a revision exercise, jot down four key points for success in:

- Writing a formal letter
- Writing a newspaper article
- Writing a description of a place
- Outlining a point of view.

Writing Wrongs

This unit will offer you an opportunity to study real examples of misfortune and injustice, past and present, to look at the responses they have inspired, and to use your skills to help people in need.
As you work through this unit you will develop your skills as:

SPEAKERS AND LISTENERS

by speaking up for victims
by discussing and debating issues
by presenting a TV news report

READERS

by encountering a range of different kinds of writing about actual
　　events including documentary accounts, pamphlets and letters
by identifying how a writer's choice of language can affect people in
　　different ways
by seeing how writing can be used to persuade people

WRITERS

by gathering ideas and by making lists, collecting examples of
　　persuasive vocabulary
by writing from somebody else's point of view
by producing material yourself aimed at stirring people into action

The events you are going to read about took place in an area of the Lake District between the village of Langdale and Grasmere in the bleak winter of 1807.

THE MAID OF GRASMERE

George and Sarah Green set forward in the forenoon of a day fated to be their last on earth. The sale was to take place in Langdalehead; to which, from their own cottage in Easedale, it was possible in daylight, and supposing no mist upon the hills, to find out a short cut of not more than eight miles. By this route they went; and, notwithstanding the snow that lay on the ground, they reached their destination in safety.

This time was considerably after sunset; and the final recollections of the crowd with respect to George and Sarah Green, were that they intended to retrace their morning path, and to attempt the perilous task of dropping down into Easedale from the mountains above Langdale Head. Party after party rode off; the meeting melted away, and, at length, nobody was left of any weight that could pretend to influence the decision of elderly people. They quitted the scene, professing to obey some advice or other upon the choice of roads; but, at as early a point as they could do so unobserved, began to ascend the hills. After this, they were seen no more. They had disappeared into the cloud of death. Voices were heard, some hours afterwards, from the mountains – voices, as some thought, of alarm; others said, no. The result was, that no attention was paid to the sounds.

That night, in little peaceful Easedale, six children sat by a peat fire, expecting the return of their parents, upon whom they depended for their daily bread. Let a day pass, and they were starved. Every sound was heard with anxiety. Every sound, every echo amongst the hills was listened to for five hours – from seven to twelve. At length, the eldest girl of the family – about nine years old – told her little brothers and sisters to go to bed. They had been taught obedience; and all of them, at the voice of their eldest sister, went off fearfully to their beds. What could be their fears, it is difficult to say; they had no knowledge to instruct them in the dangers of the hills. Some time, in the course of the evening – but it was late and after midnight – the moon arose and shed a torrent of light upon the Langdale Fells, which had already, long hours before, witnessed in darkness the death of their parents.

That night, and the following morning, came a further and a heavier fall of snow; in consequence of which the poor children were completely imprisoned, and cut off from all possibility of communicating with their next neighbours. The brook was too much for them to leap; and the little, crazy, wooden bridge could not be crossed or even approached with safety, from the drifting of the snow having made it impossible to ascertain the exact situation of some treacherous hole in its timbers, which, if trod upon, would have let a small child drop through into the rapid waters.

HOME ALONE

The writer tells us about how the children behaved whilst they were waiting for their parents to return, but 'what could be their fears, it is difficult to say'. This task is designed to help you imagine what kinds of fears you would have if you were in the same position.

- Think for a moment about the thoughts that might have been going through the children's minds. Jot down some of your initial ideas.

- In your group, imagine you are sitting round the peat fire. Give voice to the thoughts of the children. You might find it helpful to recreate the scene, sitting or standing as you think the children might have done.

- Write a script of the conversation that the children might have had that night around the fire.

Their parents did not return. For some hours of the morning, the children clung to the hope that the extreme severity of the night had tempted them to sleep in Langdale; but this hope forsook them as the day wore away. Their father, George Green, had served as a soldier, and was an active man, of ready resources, who would not, under any circumstances, have failed to force a road back to his family, had he been still living; and this reflection taught them to feel the extremity of their danger.

They huddled together in the evening round their hearth-fire of peats, and held their little councils upon what was to be done.

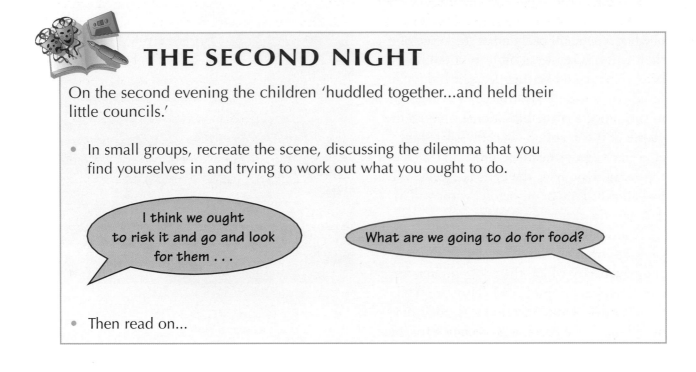

THE SECOND NIGHT

On the second evening the children 'huddled together...and held their little councils.'

- In small groups, recreate the scene, discussing the dilemma that you find yourselves in and trying to work out what you ought to do.

> I think we ought to risk it and go and look for them . . .

> What are we going to do for food?

- Then read on...

Meantime, the eldest sister, little Agnes, though sadly alarmed, and feeling the sensation of eeriness as twilight came on, she looked out from the cottage to the dreadful fells, and exerted herself to take all the measures which their own prospects made prudent. She did not fail to draw some comfort from the consideration, that the very same causes which produced their danger in one direction, sheltered them from danger of another kind – that, if they could not get out into Grasmere, on the other hand, bad men, and wild seafaring foreigners, who sometimes passed along the high road in that vale, could not get to them; and that their neighbours were kindhearted people, that would contend with each other for the privilege of assisting them.

Somewhat cheered with these thoughts,

and having caused all her brothers and sisters – except the two little things, not yet of a fit age – to kneel down and say the prayers which they had been taught, this admirable little maiden turned herself to every household task that could have proved useful to them in long captivity. First of all, upon some recollection that the clock was nearly going down, she wound it up. Next, she took all the milk which remained from what her mother had provided for the children's consumption during her absence, and for the breakfast of the following morning – this luckily was still in sufficient plenty for two days' consumption – this she took and scalded, so as to save it from turning sour. That done, she next examined the meal chest; made the common oatmeal porridge of the country, but put all of the children, except

the two youngest, on short allowance; and she found out a little hoard of flour, part of which she baked for them upon the hearth into little cakes; and this unusual delicacy persuaded them to think that they had been celebrating a feast. Next, she issued out of doors. There her first task was, with the assistance of two younger brothers, to carry in as many peats as might serve them for a week. That done, in the second place, she examined the potatoes buried in 'brackens' (that is, withered fern): these were not many; and she thought it better to leave them where they were, excepting as many as would make a single meal, under a fear that the heat of their cottage would spoil them if removed.

Then retreating into the warm house, and 'barring' the door, she sat down to undress the two youngest of the children; then she laid them carefully and cosily in their little nests up stairs, and sang them to sleep. The rest she kept up to bear her company until the clock should tell them it was midnight; up to which time she had still a lingering hope that some welcome shout from the hills above, which they were all to strain their ears to catch, might yet assure them that they were not wholly orphans, even though one parent should have perished. As last services to what she might now have called her own little family, Agnes took precautions against the drifting of the snow within the door and the imperfect window, which had caused them some discomfort on the preceding day; and, finally, she adopted elaborate plans for preventing the fire being extinguished, which would be absolutely

indispensable to their existence.

The night slipped away, and another morning came, bringing with it no better hopes of any kind. Change there had been none, but for the worse. The snow had greatly increased in quantity; and the drifts seemed far more formidable. A second day passed like the first; little Agnes still keeping all her flock quiet, and tolerably comfortable; and still calling on all the elders in succession to say their prayers, morning and night.

A third day came; and whether it was on that or on the fourth, I do not now recollect; but on one or other there came a welcome gleam of hope. The arrangement of the snow drifts had shifted during the night; and though the wooden bridge was still impracticable, a low wall had been exposed, over which it seemed possible that a road might be found into Grasmere. The little boys accompanied their sister until she came to the other side of the hill, which, lying more sheltered from the weather offered a path. Here they parted; and little Agnes pursued her mission to the nearest house she could find.

No house could have proved a wrong one in such a case. Miss Wordsworth and I often heard the description renewed, of the horror which, in an instant, displaced the smile of hospitable greeting, when little weeping Agnes told her sad tale. No tongue can express the fervid sympathy which travelled through the vale, like the fire in an American forest, when it was learned that neither George nor Sarah Green had been seen by their children since the day of the Langdale sale.

At length, dogs were taken up; and, about noonday, a shout amongst thick volumes of cloudy vapour, conveyed the news that the bodies were found. George Green was found lying at the bottom of a precipice, from which he had fallen; and, by laying together all the indications of what had passed, it was conjectured that the husband had desired his wife to pause for a few minutes, wrapping her in his own greatcoat, whilst he should go forward in order to catch a sight of some object which might ascertain their real situation. Either the snow above, already lying in drifts, or the blinding snow storms driving into his eyes, must have misled him as to the nature of the ground; for the precipice over which he had fallen was but a few yards from the spot in which he had quitted his wife. The depth of the descent, and the fury of the wind, (almost always violent on these cloudy altitudes) would prevent any distinct communication between the dying husband below and his despairing wife above; but it was believed by the shepherds that Sarah might have caught, at intervals, the groans of her unhappy partner.

Others supposed the smooth and unruffled surface of the snow where he lay seemed to argue that he had died without a struggle, perhaps without a groan, and because that tremendous sound of 'hurtling' in the upper chambers of the air, would utterly stifle any sounds so feeble as those of a dying man. In any case, it was generally agreed that the wild shrieks heard towards midnight in Langdale Head announced the agonizing moment which brought to her the conviction of utter desolation and of final abandonment. It seemed probable that the sudden disappearance of her husband from her eyes would teach her to understand his fate; had kept her stationary to the very attitude in which her husband had left her, until her failing powers and the increasing bitterness of the cold, would soon make those changes of place impossible. The footsteps in some places, wherever drifting had not obliterated them, shewed that however much they might have rambled, after crossing and doubling upon their own paths, and many a mile astray from their right track, still they must have kept together to the very shelf of rock at which their wanderings had terminated.

THE DEATHS OF GEORGE AND SARAH

- What do you find particularly tragic about the final hours of George and Sarah? Why?

- Working with a partner, choose three things described in this account that it would be particularly important to highlight in a news report of the incident.

- Prepare and present a TV news bulletin which uses a reporter on location at the scene. Your aim is to focus sympathy on the family as a whole, but especially the children. Once you have written the report, you may wish to record it on audio or video tape.

HELP

PRESENTING A TV NEWS BULLETIN

As you prepare your bulletin, try to keep the following points in mind:

- Your introduction needs to set the scene for viewers who knew nothing about the tragedy. Your aim is to 'bring the story to life'.

- News reports often contain interviews or quotations from witnesses. You might include interviews with neighbours who helped search for George and Sarah, or the person to whom Agnes first poured out the story. Remember to look back at the suggested interview techniques on page 19–20.

- TV reports are about visual impact as well as the spoken word. Where exactly is the reporter standing? What can the viewer see behind the reporter – a snow-swept hillside, the Greens' isolated cottage?

The funeral of the ill-fated Greens was attended by all the vale; it took place about eight days after they were found; and the day happened to be in the most perfect contrast to the sort of weather which prevailed at the time of their misfortune; some snow still remained here and there upon the ground; but the azure of the sky was unstained by a cloud; and a golden sunlight seemed to sleep upon the very hills where they had wandered – then a howling wilderness, but now a green pastoral lawn.

AFTER THE FUNERAL

- As a whole class, imagine that you are a group of interested adults who have just returned from George and Sarah Green's funeral and are gathering in Grasmere village hall to discuss what should be done about the children. What suggestions would emerge?

  Start in small groups discussing whether you could look after any of the children yourself and, if so, on what terms. The meeting might then become more public with one person taking responsibility for finding out what everybody thinks and starting a wider discussion.

After this solemn ceremony was over a regular distribution of the children was made amongst the wealthier families of the vale. Even the poorest had put in their claim to bear some part in the expenses of the case. But it was decided that none of the children should be entrusted to any persons who seemed likely, either from old age, or from slender means, or from personal responsibilities, to devolve the trust, sooner or later, upon strangers, who might have none of that interest in the children of the Grasmere people. Two twins, who had naturally played together and slept together from their birth, passed into the same family; the others were dispersed; but into such kind-hearted and intelligent famlies, with continual opportunities of meeting each other on errands, or at church, or at sales, that it was hard to say which had the happier fate.

And thus, in so brief a period as one fortnight, a household that, by health and strength, by the humility of poverty, and by innocence of life, seemed sheltered from all attacks but those of time, came to be utterly broken up. George and Sarah Green slept in Grasmere churchyard. Their children were scattered over wealthier houses than those of their poor parents, through the vales of Grasmere or Rydal.

The Wordsworths, meantime, were so much interested in the future fortunes and the suitable education of the children – feeling that, when both parents are suddenly cut off by a tragical death, the children become a bequest to the other members of that community – that they energetically applied themselves to the task of raising funds which in future years should carry one after another of the children into different trades or occupations; but they well understood, that more, would be raised under an immediate appeal to the sympathies of men, than if the application were delayed until the money should be needed. I have mentioned that the Royal Family were made acquainted with the details of the case; that they were powerfully affected by the story, especially by the account of little Agnes, and that they contributed most munificently.

From *Recollections of Grasmere* by De Quincey

Dear Miss Wordsworth

On hearing of the tragic death of George and Sarah Green, and of the piteous plight of their now orphaned children, please accept the enclosed donation.

We commend the benevolence of the inhabitants of Langdale, and the courage of Agnes Green and her siblings

Yours sincerely
George
His royal Majesty George III

MAKING AN APPEAL IN WRITING

It is clear from the final paragraph of the story that the Wordsworths mounted a local campaign on behalf of the children to secure their future.

- With a partner, brainstorm the various methods that they might have used to 'appeal to the sympathies of men'. Remember, it was 1807.

- Read the pamphlet below. It was published by Save the Children to raise money for starving children in Africa. Answer the questions by the arrows.

Note the personal way in which the reader is addressed.

Why do you think the letter has been headed 'Urgent'?

How has the writer used repetition to give extra force to the argument?

Some words are underlined – why?

Short sentences and short paragraphs for maximum impact.

Why have these words been chosen?

What do you notice about the type of print?

Why do you think the letter ends as it does?

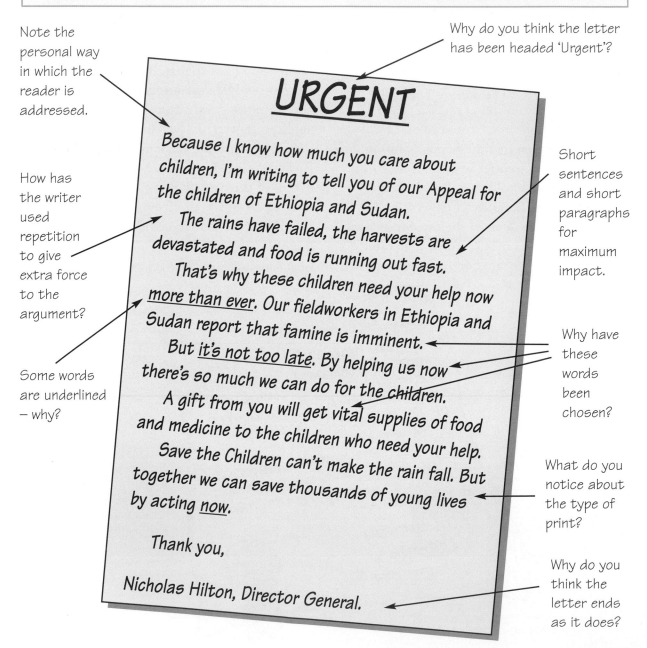

URGENT

Because I know how much you care about children, I'm writing to tell you of our Appeal for the children of Ethiopia and Sudan.

The rains have failed, the harvests are devastated and food is running out fast.

That's why these children need your help now <u>more than ever</u>. Our fieldworkers in Ethiopia and Sudan report that famine is imminent.

But <u>it's not too late</u>. By helping us now there's so much we can do for the children.

A gift from you will get vital supplies of food and medicine to the children who need your help.

Save the Children can't make the rain fall. But together we can save thousands of young lives by acting <u>now</u>.

Thank you,

Nicholas Hilton, Director General.

YOUR OWN APPEAL

On the next page, you will see an example from a national newspaper of one modern method used to gain help from the public on behalf of children. Space in the newspaper has been purchased by The Children's Society asking readers to consider adoption.

- Discuss your reaction to The Children's Society feature. What thoughts and feelings did it give you? Can you find
    facts
    words
    phrases or clause structures
that made you react in the way you did? Try to explain how the language worked on you.

- The writers have had to move people enough to consider helping, but also to warn them that this would be a serious commitment.

Find three ways in which readers are encouraged to think of adoption. Find three ways in which readers are warned that the job will be demanding.

- Now write a similar piece about the Green children. This could be either
    An appeal for families to adopt the children
    An appeal for money to support them as they grow up.

Jonathon is eight years old. He spent three difficult years in care moving from one foster family to another, unable to settle down and troubled by the bad memories of his earlier childhood. But when a family interested in adoption contacted The Children's Society and later offered him a permanent, loving home, Jonathon's life changed. He is a different boy now, happy and secure and proud of his new mum and dad.

Martin and his brother Brian lived apart for several years after their mother could no longer care for them. They are now eight and ten respectively and settling down with their new dad. He is a single person and the three of them are now the best of friends. The boys still keep in touch with their mother from time to time, an arrangement which works well with everyone.

a loving, understanding family to grow up in.

We are not looking for superman or woman, but ordinary everyday people who have one thing in common – their love of children. We are a small friendly team of adoption workers who take special pride in our training programme and in the support we offer our families. We are particularly concerned with children in the N.E region who find themselves in care through no fault of their own. Whilst we know it can be a difficult challenge, the rewards, as all our adoptive families will testify, are great.

We are looking for people from all walks of life who are interested in becoming adoptive parents for children over the age of 7 years. They may be individual children or brothers and sisters wanting to stay together, but none can return to live with their birth families and

The Children's Society

HAVE YOU ROOM IN YOUR LIFE FOR A CHILD?

There are many more success stories to tell, but sadly, still more children who have been taken into care through no fault of their own, are waiting for their special family.

This month, the Family Placement Project at the Children's Society, Billingham office hope to encourage people to come forward to talk about what it is like to adopt a child who needs

this could be their last chance of enjoying family life.

If you have the energy and commitment to care permanently for a child, we would like to hear from you. We offer full training and support. Please write or contact us for an informal chat.

The Poetry Backpack

In this unit, you will be taking a journey, during which you will collect items for a poetry 'backpack'. You will be writing your own poems and studying five poems by other poets. As you work through the unit you will develop your skills as:

SPEAKERS AND LISTENERS

by experimenting with different readings in order to see how this affects the meaning of a poem

by discussing your response to poetry

READERS

by studying the ways in which poets use language to achieve certain effects

by comparing different poems on similar themes

by looking closely at the kind of poems that are sometimes set in examinations

WRITERS

by writing your own poems

by keeping a reading journal about the poems, comparing first and subsequent impressions

by learning literary terms and defining how they work

As you turn the page you will begin your journey into poetry and will take steps to increase your knowledge of three particular themes…

Poetry is different from other kinds of writing, and it is sometimes difficult to be certain exactly what a poem is about. It can be helpful to start by identifying the 'theme' of a poem in very general terms, before defining its particular meaning any more precisely. During this unit, you will be exploring three themes:

- power
- isolation
- change

Before you begin to tackle the poems, try exploring the significance of these themes by creating a physical collage.

PHYSICAL COLLAGE

A physical collage is similar to a normal collage except that you will also appear in it. Here's what to do:

- Organise yourselves into suitable groups.

- Do some research on the three themes and see if you can find images, pictures, key words or phrases which might represent the theme you are exploring.

- Create a tableau for each of the three themes, using your bodies and the research material you have collected.

- Present these physical collages to the rest of the group (perhaps you could take photographs of them for later use) and compare how each group has 'captured' the themes.

Below is an example of a physical collage on the theme of power.

What could your group do to develop these physical collages further?

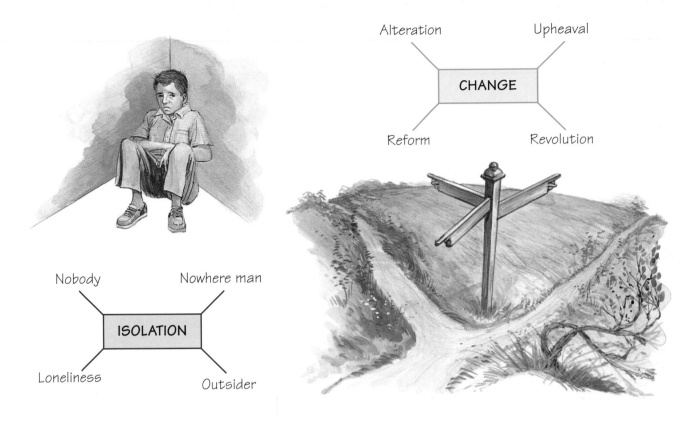

```
      Alteration        Upheaval
           \              /
            [  CHANGE  ]
           /              \
        Reform          Revolution
```

```
      Nobody        Nowhere man
          \              /
           [ ISOLATION ]
          /              \
    Loneliness         Outsider
```

YOUR OWN WRITING

A powerful way to explore these themes is through writing. You have begun your journey into poetry with three physical collages. Now take it a step further. Begin to write three poems based on the three themes: power, isolation, change.

Here are some ways to get started:

- Using three separate pages of plain paper, write down the three themes: power, isolation, change.

- On each of the pages, jot down ideas you have gained from constructing the collages.

- Try to organise these ideas into a shape or a pattern (perhaps using rhyme to begin).

- Once you have an early, rough draft, share your work in progress with your group, the class or your teacher.

- Keep these pages for inclusion in the 'backpack' that you are now going to produce.

YOUR BACKPACK

What will you need to help you make your journey into poetry? Most travellers take with them a 'backpack' of essential items for the journey. You are making a literary journey so your backpack will contain whatever you need to help you respond to and write about poetry.

Here are some suggestions for your poetry backpack:

- Make a small A5 sized booklet (kept together with treasury tags). Whatever form of binding you use, it is important to be flexible. You need to be able to add pages as you go along, expanding each section as you read new poems.

- Give the booklet a title. 'Poetry backpack' is one option, but you could choose something else – 'A Rough Guide to Poetry', for example, or 'Poetry Made Plain'.

- Create a **first section** called 'What is poetry?'. Leave enough space to return to this page with new ideas, but start the booklet by noting what you currently know and think about poetry.

- Reserve a number of pages, as **Section 2**, for examples of the techniques poets use:
    images: metaphor and simile
    symbolism
    sounds: alliteration, assonance and onomatopoeia
    structure
    narrative
    the narrator
    setting
    rhythm and rhyme

- For **Section 3**, design a page which will help you make rough notes on individual poems. You might want to create a space for first impressions, or include some general headings such as 'theme' or 'techniques'.

- Finally, for **Section 4**, leave space for developing your own anthology. This might include poems that you particularly like, or song lyrics or other poems on the three themes covered in this unit. Your own poems will also be included here.

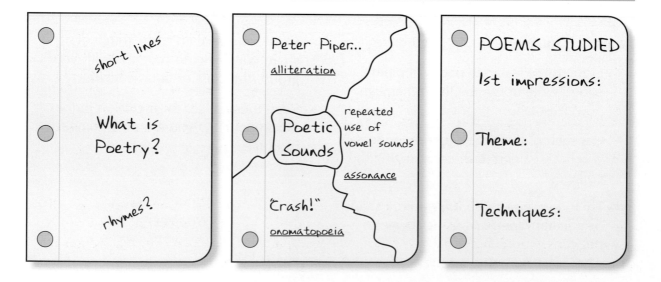

FRAGMENTS

You are now going to study poems on each of the three themes.
The first theme you will be exploring is 'Power'.

The sun is behind me.
Nothing has changed since I began.
My eye has permitted no change.
I am going to keep things like this.

The convenience of the high trees!
The air's boyancy and the sun's ray
Are of advantage to me;
and the earth's face upward for my inspection.

Two vast and trunkless legs of stone
Stand in the desert...

'My name is Ozymandias, king of kings:
Look on my works, ye Mighty, and despair!'

I sit in the top of the wood, my eyes closed.
Inaction, no falsifying dream
Between my hooked head and hooked feet:
Or in sleep rehearse perfect kills and eat.

Nothing beside remains. Round the decay
Of that colossal wreck, boundless and bare
The lone and level sands stretch far away.

The allotment of death.
For the one path of my flight is direct
Through the bones of the living.
No arguments assert my right:

Near them, on the sand,
Half sunk, a shattered visage lies, whose frown,
And wrinkled lip, and sneer of cold command,
Tell that its sculptor well those passions read
Which yet survive, stamped on these lifeless things,

The hand that mocked them, and the heart that fed:

My feet are locked upon the rough bark.
It took the whole of Creation
To produce my foot, my each feather:
Now I hold Creation in my foot

Or fly up, and revolve it all slowly–
I kill where I please because it is all mine.
There is no sophistry in my body:
My manners are tearing off heads–

I met a traveller from an antique land
Who said:

And on the pedestal these words appear:

CONNECTIONS

The fragments above, from two different poems, have been placed on the page in an entirely random fashion. Before sorting them out, see if you can find any links between them.

You can do this in two different ways:

1 Work in pairs and read each of the fragments. Find as many connections as you can between the different coloured extracts and record these on a piece of

paper that is large enough to be displayed around the room, or:

2 Ask your teacher to copy the page and randomly hand out a fragment to each member of the class. On a given signal, pair up with someone with a differently coloured extract. Read each others' and find a connection. Be as creative as you can with your connections. List everyone's ideas on a piece of paper for display.

You have been involved, hopefully, in an exercise designed to get you to make original connections between two very different texts. As you start preparing for examination work in the future, you will find that you are frequently asked to compare and contrast different poems on similar themes.

POETRY JIGSAW

Now you need to look at each of the poems individually. First though, see if you can sort the fragments into an order which makes sense to you. Make sure you can justify the sequence! This should help you to discover something about the way in which each of the poems has been written.

Although there is clearly a 'right' sequence, your teacher will be more interested in your reasons than in whether your order is correct.

You might find the following framework useful:

- Read through the jigsaw pieces in a pair or small group.

- Look carefully at the punctuation used to see if it gives you any clues about the order.

- Read over some of the sections three or four times and look for more clues to tell you how each one is connected to the next.

- Use the following format to record your thinking:

  The section on _____ is connected to the section on _____ because _____
  (repeat this as often as necessary)

Now, add to the pages in Section 2 of your backpack by highlighting:

- Structure – What did you notice about the way the poems were put together?

- Imagery – What can you say about the way in which imagery is used in the poem?

- Sound – How does the sound of the words contribute to the meaning of the poem?

OZYMANDIAS

The first poem is called 'Ozymandias' and is by Percy Shelley, a writer who lived in the early 19th century. His wife, Mary, wrote 'Frankenstein'.

I met a traveller from an antique land

Who said: Two vast and trunkless legs of stone

Stand in the desert...Near them, on the sand,

Half sunk, a shattered visage lies, whose frown,

And wrinkled lip, and sneer of cold command,

Tell that its sculptor well those passions read

Which yet survive, stamped on these lifeless things,

The hand that mocked them, and the heart that fed:

And on the pedestal these words appear:

'My name is Ozymandias, king of kings:

Look on my works, ye Mighty, and despair!'

Nothing beside remains. Round the decay

Of that colossal wreck, boundless and bare

The lone and level sands stretch far away.

READINGS

Reading aloud in pairs or groups allows you to experience the poem and to come to a more considered judgement about it. Try reading Ozymandias in groups of three:

- One person to read the words you feel that the poet is speaking
- One person to read the words of the traveller
- One person to read the words of the king himself.

INTERPRETATIONS

Study the inscription on the pedestal of the king and read the words aloud again.
What do you think the following people would say that it meant?

- Ozymandias himself
- The sculptor who made the statue and carved the words
- Other people living at the time of Ozymandias
- The traveller who heard about it

Using large pieces of paper, and working in pairs, select specific images from the poem. Do a rough sketch to illustrate each, and then explain what they suggest to you. Finally, move on to what it reminds you of in our world today. What relevance does it have?

An example has been done for you.

'Sneer of cold command'

cruelty, power, control,
heartlessness, authority,
superior manner,
looks down on others,
knows he will be obeyed.

HAWK ROOSTING

The second poem you tried to piece together in the poetry jigsaw
was Hawk Roosting by Ted Hughes.

I sit in the top of the wood, my eyes closed.
Inaction, no falsifying dream
Between my hooked head and hooked feet:
Or in sleep rehearse perfect kills and eat.

The convenience of the high trees!
The air's buoyancy and the sun's ray
Are of advantage to me;
And the earth's face upward for my inspection.

My feet are locked upon the rough bark.
It took the whole of Creation
To produce my foot, my each feather:
Now I hold Creation in my foot.

Or fly up, and revolve it all slowly–
I kill where I please because it is all mine.
There is no sophistry in my body:
My manners are tearing off heads–

The allotment of death.
For the one path of my flight is direct
Through the bones of the living.
No arguments assert my right:

The sun is behind me.
Nothing has changed since I began.
My eye has permitted no change.
I am going to keep things like this.

Ted Hughes

READINGS

Read around the class, moving to the
next reader each time you reach a
punctuation mark.

Try adding different 'tones' to your
class reading. Which might work? What
about varying your voice level and
adding or removing emotion? What
effect does this have on your
understanding of the hawk?

INTERPRETATIONS

Who am I?

- As a whole group, discuss and collect ideas about the type of character the voice in the poem suggests. What emotions does this character possess? What would be their age and occupation? Is this character actually a person, or could it represent an abstract idea?

- Split into groups of three or four. Take one idea from those suggested in your discussion. Go back to the poem and find specific words that back up your theory and justify it. Now repeat this with two more ideas.

HAWK ROOSTING

IDEA
We think it sounds as if:

- The voice is that of a contract killer – a 'hitman'
-
-

QUOTATIONS
These quotations suggest this:

- 'rehearse perfect kills'
-
-

EXPLANATIONS

- It sounds as if he has become obsessed with killing
-
-

You've explored the two poems, found links between them and discussed possible interpretations. Now you are going to record some of your observations in your backpack:

The following terms are often used when discussing poetry.

Structure: The way a poem is organised – how it is built up into its final shape.

Narrative: The story or plot – the events and what happens in the poem.

Narrator: Who is actually telling the story/giving the message in the poem.

Symbolism: Something which stands for or represents something else.

Setting: Where the events in the poem take place.

Context: The social, cultural or historical background of the poem.

- There should already exist a section in your backpack for each of these terms. Under each heading, copy out the definition included above and put down your own comments on what you think it means. You might want to select some quotations from the poems you have read, explaining how they work. Include your own response, commenting particularly on whether the extracts you have chosen achieve the effect that the writer intended. Don't be afraid to record anything that occurs to you, even if you are a bit uncertain about it.

- Finally, at the end of each section, see if you can provide a better definition of the term than the one you have been given here.

- Also use this opportunity to add more notes to your existing pages on imagery and sound by recording specific examples from these two poems.

YOUR OWN POEMS

Now return to your own early drafts based on the three themes of power, isolation and change. Find your draft of a poem on the theme of 'Power'. See if you can begin a re-draft which uses some of the techniques you have discovered in these two poems. You may wish to add examples of symbolism or alliteration to your original.

What setting, character, creature or symbol could you use to further develop your poem and your understanding of the concept of power?

surround me,
Gun shots ~~firing all over~~

constantly moving
~~So I move~~ to stay undercover.

      screeches
~~I hear~~ a bird ~~tweet~~ and ^ flies away

Silence invades the air.
^Not a sound ^ is made.

Keep still ~~remember~~ and hold ~~your~~ breath
      prey
~~as you~~ search for ~~someone to kill~~.

At the beginning of this unit you were asked to explore three separate themes, producing a physical collage on each and then making a first attempt at a piece of poetry on each of them. Look back at your work on the theme of isolation. The next section of this unit deals with two poems about human isolation.

EXCAVATION

Reading poetry can be a little bit like being an archeologist because you are searching among the words for clues about what the writers or the texts are trying to say.

Imagine that you are an archeologist and that you have unearthed the text overleaf. You are going to investigate this document to see what you can piece together from the evidence it offers.

One method of investigating is to breathe life into the long hidden poem by reading it aloud. However, you have no idea how the poet intended it to be read so you will have to experiment.

Try a number of different approaches:

- Work in pairs and read through the poem. You will notice straight away that the poem is structured in seven small verses each of which rhyme. These are called rhyming couplets.

- Take one of the rhyming couplets. You are going to share the reading of each line. Decide where your partner will start and where you will take over. Will it be after two words, three words? How will you decide where to separate each line? When you have made this decision, apply it to all of the rhyming couplets.

- Now read it aloud. What do you notice about the way the lines are balanced? Do you notice anything about the use of punctuation?

- Try reading it in a different way using a variety of voices. There are a number of characters' names mentioned in the poem. Provide each of them with a different voice and read through the poem again. What changes do you notice?

What do you learn about the poem from these readings and why has it been written?

Over the heather the wet wind blows,
I've lice in my tunic and a cold in my nose.

The rain comes pattering out of the sky,
I'm a Wall soldier, I don't know why.

The mist creeps over the hard grey stone,
My girl's in Tungria; I sleep alone.

Aulus goes hanging around her place,
I don't like his manners, I don't like his face.

Piso's a Christian, he worships a fish;
There'd be no kissing if he had his wish.

She gave me a ring but I diced it away;
I want my girl and I want my pay.

When I'm a veteran with only one eye
I shall do nothing but look at the sky.

W. H. Auden

RECONSTRUCTION

Clearly the poem is spoken by somebody who is feeling very lonely. Who might he be?

As the archeologist, you have found a skull alongside the poem and you've been given the job of reconstructing the face.

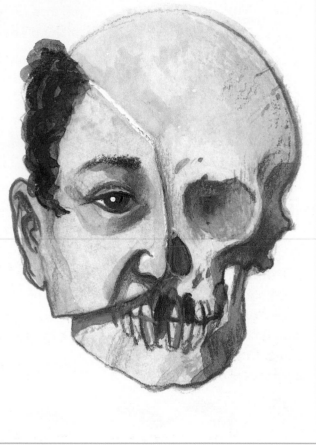

- Get yourself a large piece of blank paper and copy on to it the skull in the diagram opposite. You are going to use this skull to reconstruct the personality of the character in the poem. Instead of clay to re-model the face, you will be using words from the poem which you think put flesh on the bones of his situation, his emotions and thoughts and what matters in his life.

- Around the outside of the skull, place the words and phrases from the poem which you think capture his moods and thoughts.

- At the bottom of the piece of paper, leave a section to write a brief extract from your archeological report. This extract should explain your findings. It should concentrate on the evidence you have uncovered in the poem and the conclusions you have drawn from them.

WRITING YOUR ARCHEOLOGICAL REPORT

A way of collecting evidence and recording your findings is suggested below:

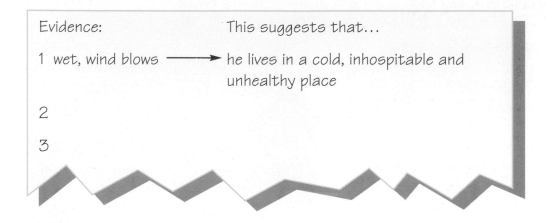

Evidence: This suggests that...

1 wet, wind blows ——————→ he lives in a cold, inhospitable and
                             unhealthy place

2

3

Perhaps you could conclude your report like this:

From the evidence uncovered in the text it can be inferred that
the man in question lived in an exposed and unhealthy area. It is
possible to deduce this from his use of the words: 'wet, wind
blows' and the fact that he seems to suffer from colds. Perhaps
his clothing was inappropriate? He only seems to be wearing a
tunic. Does this suggest that he does not know local customs
and dress?

Remember to include this work in your poetry backpack.

This poem was actually called Roman Wall Blues and it was written in the 20th century by W. H. Auden, the same poet who wrote 'Stop all the Clocks' – made famous in the film *Four Weddings and a Funeral*.

RESEARCH

- What are 'the blues'? Do some research of your own and find out what the term means. You could try a dictionary or a reference book in your library as a starting point.

- Auden also wrote a poem called 'Refugee Blues' – see if you can find it and compare it to Roman Wall Blues. What similarities and differences can you find?

- The term 'blues' also refers to a style of music. In your research, try to find information about the blues: the type of music it is, where it comes from and why it has been called 'the blues'.

Leadbelly

"Leavin', leavin'
I'm leavin' in the morning
and I don' know where to go.
Woman I bin livin' with for twenty years
Sez I can't stay here no more."

RHYTHM AND RHYME

From your readings and study of 'Roman Wall Blues', you will have noticed the strong emphasis on rhythm and rhyme common to most blues lyrics.

- In your backpack, jot down what you have found out about rhyming couplets, and the rhythm used in this poem to bring out the sadness and the pathos of the character.

- An interesting way to really understand how rhythm and rhyme work in poetry is to apply the techniques to your own version. Look back to your poem on 'isolation' in the backpack. Experiment with your ideas by including some of Auden's techniques. Try especially to focus on a blues style with the regular rhythmic drive that he uses.

THE MAN IN THE BOWLER HAT

Another poem which tackles the theme of 'isolation' is 'The Man in the Bowler Hat' by A.S.J. Tessimond.

The Man in the Bowler Hat

I am the unnoticed, the unnoticeable man:
The man who sat on your right in the morning train:
The man you looked through like a windowpane:
The man who was the colour of the carriage, the colour of
   the mounting
Morning pipe smoke.

I am the man too busy with a living to live,
Too hurried and worried to see and smell and touch:
The man who is patient too long and obeys too much
And wishes too softly and seldom.

I am the man they call the nation's backbone,
Who am boneless – playable catgut, pliable clay:
The Man they label Little lest one day
I dare to grow.

I am the rails on which the moment passes,
The megaphone for many words and voices:
I am graph, diagram,
Composite face.

I am the led, the easily-fed,
The tool, the not-quite-fool,
The would-be-safe-and-sound,
The uncomplaining, bound,
The dust fine-ground,
Stone-for-a-statue waveworn pebble-round.

READINGS

In order to explore and gain an understanding of this poem, you could prepare a dramatic enactment to present to the rest of the group. Initially, you will need to organise yourselves into groups of four or five with the poem in front of you and a large piece of blank paper for your ideas.

A dramatic enactment of the poem means that in your groups, you will need to:

- Look carefully at each of the five verses and come to an agreed understanding of them.

- Decide on how each verse could be performed and narrated.

- Organise props, costumes and sound effects.

- Rehearse and carefully craft your presentation to gain the maximum effect.

Try to consider original ways of interpreting the poem.
    During your rehearsals, keep returning to the poem. Pay particular attention to the way the punctuation guides you to use pauses. A moment's silence, at a chosen point can be very powerful.
    How will you shape your presentation?

- You could use a volunteer to sit in the middle of your group while others move around reading the words.

- You could 'thought-track' the person in the middle and give voice to his/her inner-most thoughts.

Return to your backpack and add to your section on symbols. What does the man in the bowler hat stand for? How relevant is he to life at the beginning of the new millennium?

WRITE ON

You are going to try your hand at an 'I am…' poem. Look at the picture. It is by a famous artist called Rene Magritte. What ideas does this give you? What sort of person might be painted using symbols such as this?

To try your own 'I am…' poem, follow these suggestions:

- Think of a person in society who is different in some way.

- Jot down words which describe their appearance, where they live, how they feel.

- Create a dilemma or crisis that the person might be involved in.

- Try writing a verse using some of the techniques and structures you have already learnt about.

"*The Son of Man*, 1964, by Rene Magritte"

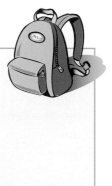

POETIC TERMS

This would also be a good moment to add pages in your backpack on imagery, symbolism, sound and structure. Quickly glance back over the work you have done in isolation. What poetic terms have you covered? What examples can you find to add to your backpack?

MAKING COMPARISONS

This page asks you to stand back and take an objective view of 'Roman Wall Blues' and 'The Man in the Bowler Hat'. Look at the table below. Work in small groups and lay out a page of blank paper in the same way, with 'Similarities' at the top of one column and 'Differences' at the top of the other.

Now look back over the two poems. What similarities and differences can you find?

Place your responses in the appropriate column and choose someone in your group to feed back your ideas to the rest of your class.

Roman Wall Blues and The Man in the Bowler Hat

	SIMILARITIES	DIFFERENCES
Content:	• Both poems deal with an isolated individual. • • •	• • • One is set in the distant past, one in the 20th century. •
Themes:	• Isolation • • • •	• One is particular, one is universal. • • •
Poetic techniques:	• • • • •	• • • R.W.B. has rhyming couplets. M.I.B.H. has more lines to each verse.
Feelings:	• • • • •	• • • • •

A very common theme in poetry is that of 'change'. It was the third theme in your series of physical collages and it is the final one to be considered. Look back at what you had to say on the theme of change in your earlier work.

A HARD RAIN'S A-GONNA FALL

In order to connect your own experiences of change and upheaval to those in the poem, it is necessary to bring them to mind.

- Look at the series of images in the background on this page and think about the events happening in the world which have been a backdrop to your life. What seem to you to be the significant events, turning points and changes during your life? Make a list.

- Now look at the questions superimposed over the images and discuss your responses to them.

Where have you been? (What are the most significant places in your life?)

What have you seen? (Which images from your past stick in your mind?)

What did you hear? (Can you think of sounds which bring to mind a memory?)

Who did you meet? (Who are the people who have most influenced you?)

What'll you do now? (Having had those experiences, what will you do with your life?)

When you have finished, read the poem on the opposite page.

A Hard Rain's A-Gonna Fall

Oh, where have you been, my blue-eyed son?
Oh, where have you been, my darling young one?
I've stumbled on the side of twelve misty mountains,
I've walked and I've crawled on six crooked highways,
I've stepped in the middle of seven sad forests,
I've been out in front of a dozen dead oceans,
I've been ten thousand miles in the mouth of a graveyard,
And it's a hard, and it's a hard, it's a hard, and it's a hard,
And it's a hard rain's a-gonna fall.

Oh, what did you see, my blue-eyed son?
Oh, what did you see, my darling young one?
I saw a newborn baby with wild wolves all around it,
I saw a highway of diamonds with nobody on it,
I saw a black branch with blood that kept drippin',
I saw a room full of men with their hammers a-bleedin',
I saw a white ladder all covered with water,
I saw ten thousand talkers whose tongues were all broken,
I saw guns and sharp swords in the hands of young children,
And it's a hard, and it's a hard, it's a hard, it's a hard,
And it's a hard rain's a-gonna fall.

And what did you hear, my blue-eyed son?
And what did you hear, my darling young one?
I heard the sound of a thunder, it roared out a warnin',
Heard the roar of a wave that could drown the whole world,
Heard one hundred drummers whose hands were a-blazin',
Heard ten thousand whisperin' and nobody listenin',
Heard one person starve, I heard many people laughin',
Heard the song of a poet who died in the gutter,
Heard the sound of a clown who cried in the alley,
And it's a hard, and it's a hard, it's a hard, it's a hard,
And it's a hard rain's a-gonna fall.

Oh, who did you meet, my blue-eyed son?
Who did you meet, my darling young one?
I met a young child beside a dead pony,
I met a white man who walked a black dog,
I met a young woman whose body was burning,
I met a young girl, she gave me a rainbow,
I met one man who was wounded in love,
I met another man who was wounded with hatred,
And it's a hard, it's a hard, it's a hard, it's a hard,
It's a hard rain's a-gonna fall.

Oh, what'll you do now, my blue-eyed son?
Oh, what'll you do now, my darling young one?
I'm a-going' back out 'fore the rain starts a-fallin',
I'll walk to the depths of the deepest black forest,
Where the people are many and their hands are all empty,
Where the pellets of poison are flooding their waters,
Where the home in the valley meets the damp dirty prison,
Where the executioner's face is always well hidden,
Where hunger is ugly, where souls are forgotten,
Where black is the color, where none is the number,
And I'll tell it and think it and speak it and breathe it,
And reflect it from the mountain so all souls can see it,
Then I'll stand on the ocean until I start sinkin',
But I'll know my song well before I start singin',
And it's a hard, it's a hard, it's a hard, it's a hard,
It's a hard rain's a-gonna fall.

READINGS

This poem contains two voices and is in the form of a dialogue with the older (father figure?) asking questions and the younger voice answering them.

- Try reading it in this way by having one person take on the role of the older person and the rest of the class sharing the responses to the five basic questions as asked on the previous page.

- You might like to allocate a line to each person in the class and ask them to decide how they would deliver their reply. Would it be defiantly, in a timid way, fearfully or even in a bragging manner?

CONSIDERING THE POEM

In groups, consider the following questions:

- What sort of people and places has he seen?

- What do you think the chorus of 'hard rain' means?

- What does the son think of the world he has witnessed?

- How would you explain what he's going to go back out and do?

PICTURES, IMAGES, METAPHORS

- Working on your own, choose two images from each stanza, copy the words out and sketch their meaning on a blank sheet of paper. This should give you ten images from the poem.

- Next to each of these images, write a sentence explaining what it might mean.

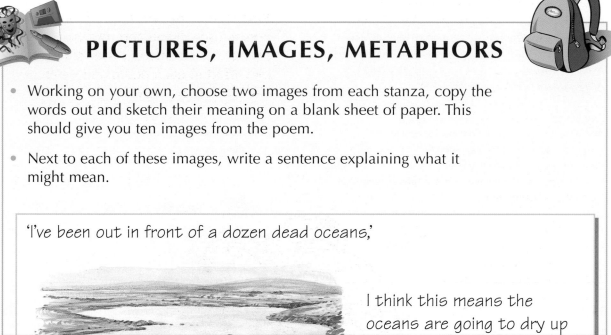

'I've been out in front of a dozen dead oceans,'

I think this means the oceans are going to dry up because of global warming.

By explaining what you think each image means, you are, in fact, interpreting the metaphors.

Add to your backpack any ideas you have formed about images and metaphors and how they affect your understanding of poems.

You have now completed your journey of exploration through a number of poems which deal with the issues of power, isolation and change. In doing so, you have collected a wide variety of quotes and ideas which should have helped you understand how poetry works.

UNPACKING

Rummage through the backpack one last time and see if you can complete your sections on:

Structure: provide examples of how each of the poems is put together differently.

Imagery/symbolism: make sure that you have recorded the different ways in which images are used and what they stand for.

Rhyme and rhythm: each of these poems uses rhyme and rhythm differently for different effects. How are they used in each poem and what effects do they achieve?

USING YOUR KNOWLEDGE

Now it's time to finalise your creative pieces armed with the knowledge about poetry you have acquired along the way.

For your final drafts, how are you going to shape your poems on Power, Isolation and Change?

More to the point, what are you going to do with them? Poems need a reader to bring them to life. When you have finished your final drafts, you will need an audience. You could obviously use your teacher or your group but it is far more dangerous and satisfying to take your poems to a wider audience.

WHAT NEXT?

If you are feeling brave, you could:

- **Create a bulletin board**. If your school has an Internet site, you could create some new pages on which to 'publish' your poems, with illustrations.

- **Publish an anthology**. It is not difficult to publish your own anthology, using appropriate software, scanning in illustrations and photocopying the result.

- **Organise a lunchtime reading**. One of the most effective ways of presenting poetry is in conjunction with music. Find some music or sounds that are appropriate to the poems you have written and organise a lunchtime reading. Create your own 'Edinburgh Festival'.

- **Look at local newspapers**. In some parts of the country, the local newspaper occasionally devotes a few pages to local writing. See if you can get your work included.

- **E-mail another school**. Your school may already have e-mail links with schools elsewhere. Use the e-mail link to share your poems with another class elsewhere and invite responses.